Coffeehouse Compatibilism

Coffeehouse Compatibilism

The Espresso that Drowned an Idea

David S. Lahm

RESOURCE *Publications* · Eugene, Oregon

COFFEEHOUSE COMPATIBILISM
The Espresso that Drowned an Idea

Resource Publications
An Imprint of Wipf and Stock Publishers
199 W. 8th Ave., Suite 3
Eugene, OR 97401
www.wipfandstock.com

ISBN 13: 978-1-62032-575-9
Manufactured in the U.S.A.

"Ours is the great teacher of all wisdom, and the whole world, including Athens and Greece, belongs to Him."

-IGNATIUS OF ANTIOCH

Contents

Foreword

THE QUESTION OF FREEDOM is one of the most perplexing, yet existentially engaging issues that has ever preoccupied human beings. This issue crosses ideological divides, and is an urgent one for both philosophers and theologians, for those who believe in God as well as those who believe the material world is all that exists.

Freedom has been a central concern in the broader human enterprise for a number of reasons. Indeed, the assumption that human beings are free has been essential to the traditional notion of human dignity, as suggested by the famous title of B. F. Skinner's book *Beyond Freedom and Dignity*. When belief in freedom wanes, so do traditional convictions about the exalted significance of our choices, if not our very lives. Moreover, much of traditional morality, including our legal system, has taken for granted that human beings are free and responsible for their actions.

While the stakes are enormously high for even secular philosophers for these sorts of reasons, they are even higher in a theological context where the ultimate measure of the significance and consequences of our choices is a God of holy love. With the alternatives of eternal happiness or misery, salvation or damnation in view, the stakes are raised dramatically. In this context, the question about freedom is the pressing one of whether salvation is genuinely available for all persons. Is it the case that any who are lost end up separated from God only because they freely persisted in rejecting his grace, or does God simply choose to leave some people in sin, so they never have the freedom to accept his grace and be saved? These questions are energetically debated in the church today, largely due to the resurgence of Calvinism, particularly among the younger generation, and the interest in this classic theological controversy does not appear to be going away any time soon.

David Lahm has written an engaging and informative book that will introduce you to a number of the key philosophical and theological issues, and moreover, put you squarely in the middle of the debate. I would encourage readers to enter the coffee shop fully aware that the issues served up are hot. As you listen in, you will not only enjoy the debate, but will find yourself taking sides, and when you finally leave, you will better understand why you do, and why it matters.

Jerry L. Walls
Professor of Philosophy
Houston Baptist University

Preface

THIS BOOK IS A philosophical dialogue about the issue of free will for Christians. Now, I know what you're thinking— I'm a reader too, you know. If I could capture your sarcastic inner monologue in print (shame on you!), it might read something like this: "Come on! Another book about freedom, another manuscript on the possibility of a contra-causal will? Hasn't every philosopher, theologian, and his mother's brother written on this topic? This is a paragon of redundancy, if there ever was one. The title of the work would more aptly read,

'An invitation to kick a dead horse.'"

Okay, okay, point taken. But I think you'll be happy to know that, as far as I can see it, this work differs in at least 3 ways from other similarly focused books:.

1. Being a dialogue, I hope you will find the delivery much more entertaining and engaging than a classical philosophy textbook.

2. The book focuses on the philosophy of the free will debate, with the integration of Christian theology and biblical studies (in the final chapter). This integration of observations and arguments from the different fields gives the work its most differentiating feature.

3. Finally, although this book does recapitulate the philosophical free will debate for the Christian thinker,

it also offers some radically new thoughts and arguments pertinent to the Arminian/Calvinist debate.

Some of the questions we will cover are the following:.

- Are we free?

- What is '*freedom*'?

- What impact would it have if we weren't?

- Is it possible that we are determined, and yet free in a sense too?

- Is there any way we can know?

- How does all this fit into our Christian faith?

So, if you've ever wondered over breakfast whether or not your choice of cereal that morning was at the end of some causal chain or—worse yet—if you've ever wondered whether or not your *action of wondering* about whether or not your choice of cereal this morning was at the end of a causal chain was itself at the end of a causal chain, come and join our discussion.[1] You are just the type, inquisitive and thoughtful, that will enjoy listening in on the conversation of our three academics – Calvin, Wesley, and B.F.

It is my sincere hope within the pages of this text that you, the reader, will find murky waters cleared, monotonous logic rendered enjoyable, and, at least in some small respect, come to appreciate the gravity and ubiquity of this prevailing and fundamental philosophical issue: the freedom of the will.

1. Here is a different way of saying the same thing, "Have you ever wondered about whether or not one of your actions was determined (e.g. your choice of breakfast cereal this morning, or the lie you told your boss last week)? Now, what if that very action of wondering about your former choice was determined? What if it was a determined event that you wonder about whether or not you are determined, or about whether or not some specific action that you have done was determined?"

Acknowledgments

THIS BOOK WOULD NOT have been written without the constant encouragement of my sweet wife Rachel. She is an inspiration to me and my closest and dearest companion. In addition, I would like to extend special thanks to the Philosophy and Religion department at Liberty University, and most particularly to Dr. David Baggett. It is under the tutelage of Dr. Baggett, and in the care of his guiding friendship, that I gained the vision of writing this book. His candor, humility, and passion for philosophy continue to inspire me.

Introduction

*Sometimes the questions are complicated
and the answers are simple.*

—DR. SEUSS

Most men would rather die than think. Many do.

—BERTRAND RUSSELL

THROUGHOUT HISTORY, PEOPLE HAVE wondered whether or not they were free; free to do as they wish, and wish as they wish.[1] Many have supposed that all of their actions might be determined, either by fate, God, physical laws, their own genetic make-up, the laws of logic, social conditioning, demonic activity, or even the recent horoscope. This fear can be represented by a passage from Charles Dickens, *A Christmas Carol*,

> The spirit stood among the graves, and pointed down to one. He advanced towards it, trembling. The phantom was exactly as it had been, but he dreaded that he saw new meaning in

---

1. The question of freedom is twofold. First, can people do as they want (1st order desire)? Second, can they want what they want (2nd order desire)? This distinction will become clearer as the dialogue progresses.

its solemn shape. "Before I draw nearer to that stone to which you point," said Scrooge, "answer me one question. Are these the shadows of the things that *will be*, or are they the shadows of the things that *may be*, only?" Still the ghost pointed downward to the grave by which it stood. "Men's courses will foreshadow certain ends, to which, if persevered in, they must lead," said Scrooge. "But if the courses be departed from, the ends will change. Say it is thus with what you show me!" The spirit was immovable as ever.[2]

Thus, Scrooge's question, and ours, can be stated as a simple dichotomy,

(#1) "Are we free or are we determined?"

In Scrooge's case, he wanted to know whether or not his somber future was fixed, such that he could not alter it. It has largely been assumed (not just by Scrooge), in thinking about question #1, that if people discovered that they were in fact free, or had "free wills," then they would be, by default, not determined. Or, stated in the opposite, if people ascertained, by reasoning or even scientific experimentation, that all of their actions were determined to happen, then this would provide sufficient reason to deny that they were free. It seems that Scrooge accepted this dichotomy (#1).

However, not all share Scrooge's assumptions. In fact, (#1) is no longer the sole or main controversy within philosophical circles.[3] The new question goes deeper. It asks,

2. Charles Dickens. *A Christmas Carol*, (London: Hodder & Stoughton), 121.

3. "The main contested question in current discussions of free will is not, as one might expect, whether or not we have free will. It is

(#2) "If we are determined, and who knows whether we are or not[4], is this compatible with being free? Can there be freedom in a deterministic universe?"

Whereas question #1 assumed an irremediable dichotomy between determinism and free will, question #2 assumes nothing. If freedom can be defined in such a way that it is harmonious with determinism, then we have answered question #1; the answer is "yes."

Obviously, there are different schools of thought on both of these questions, and different nuances within the respective viewpoints. However, the chart below will give you a very general overview as we begin, outlining the basic landscape.

	Are we free?	Is free will compatible with Determinism?	Is Determinism true?
Determinist	No	No	Yes
Libertarian	Yes	No	No
Compatibilist[5]	Yes	Yes	Maybe

---

whether or not free will is compatible with determinism." Peter Van Inwagen, *An Essay on Free Will*, (Oxford: Clarendon Press, 1985), 55.

4. Compatibilist John Martin Fischer says that compatibilism, as such, need not take a stance on the truth or falsity of determinism. Robert Kane, John Martin Fischer, Derk Pereboom, Manuel Vargas, *Four Views on Free Will*, (Blackwell, 2007), 44.

5. Compatibilism may also be called soft-determinism. Likewise, determinism may go by hard-determinism.

In the dialogue that follows, B.F. will be representing Determinism, Wesley will stand for the Libertarian viewpoint, and Calvin will be our Compatibilist. However, one last tidying-up of terms is in order before we begin.

When we hear the word 'freedom,' many things come to mind. In America, we automatically brood over phrases like "freedom of the press," "freedom of religion," "freedom from want," or even the electric coda of the late Dr. Martin Luther King Jr's famous speech, ". . . free at last, free at last, thank God almighty we are free at last." In Christian circles, there is much talk about the biblical doctrines of "freedom from sin" and "Christian liberty." There are the ideas of being free from addiction and free from past psychologically debilitating traumas (i.e. "I am free from it now. I have forgiven him.") Also, many would think of freedom in terms of doing as you please, which could differ in degree from person to person, depending on such things as wealth and extra time. So, there are various uses of the word 'freedom.' However, the variety of freedom that will be discussed in the following pages is the freedom necessary for moral and rational responsibility.[6] The questions we will ask ourselves are (1) what type of freedom[7] would it take to make sense of

6. J.P. Moreland & William Lane Craig, *Philosophical Foundations for a Christian Worldview*, (Downers Grove: Intervarsity Press, 2003), 268. Robert Kane, John Martin Fischer, Derk Pereboom, Manuel Vargas, *Four Views on Free Will*, (Blackwell, 2007), 1.

7. As you go deeper into the study of this topic, you will realize that there are many ways to understand the word "freedom" even in this further, limited sense. Should our freedom be understood as: a type of ability [cf. Peter Van Inwagen, *An Essay on Free Will*, 9-10], a state that we are in when we are free from external and internal compulsion (dictator, slave driver, mind controller/ irresistible addiction), or a state that we are in when our 2nd and 1st order desires coincide [cf. Harry Frankfurt, "Freedom of the Will and the Concept of a Person," in Gary Watson ed., *Free Will*, (Oxford: University press, 2003), 333]?

our ideas about being responsible for our actions, desires, and thoughts? And (2) do we have this freedom? Of course, as with all other philosophical debates, there are questions behind these two questions; and further questions, even more fundamental, behind them and so on and so forth ad infinitum.[8] One such question could be, is good and evil just human perception? Well, it is not within the purview of this book to prove to you the truth of,

"I am a person with a moral responsibility to my fellow man and to God."

Descartes had enough on his plate with just the first two words of that statement. No, I am a Christian and, as such, will assume a Christian worldview in what follows. This includes an affirmation of the truth and objectivity of morality. Moreover, in my opinion, morality has historically been the fuel whereby the furnace of this debate has kept so hot throughout the ages. Yes, because this debate touches upon our moral self-understanding, it has stirred us to further reflection. It has made us angry. It has shaken the foundations of our intellectual house; and I hope that going forward, you will see some of those foundations more clearly. I hope you will perceive what parts of the house they support and upon which floorboards it is safe to walk.

Socrates once said, "Wisdom begins with wonder." Since the beginning of time, no one has ever attempted to read a book on the philosophical notion of freedom, unless that person was enthralled by the puzzle (. . . or enrolled in Philosophy 101). The free will puzzle is problematic, multifaceted, and just plain tough, but it is also mesmerizing and bleeds into every other area of philosophical discussion. A good handle on the issue of free will can provide direction on many other questions ranging from theological to political. This study will be no walk in the park. However,

8. Latin phrase meaning "to infinity."

such a weighty issue deserves your attention and deliberation and you will be all the better for it. I, therefore, heartily recommend that you grab yourself a caffeinated beverage, a pencil, and your thinking-cap, and dive into what should be a riveting and humorous intellectual exchange. Don't suffocate yourself in B.F.'s moustache or be frightened by Calvin's austerity. Stay the course. It's worth it.

The Gathering

Three Schools Collide

A man's character may be learned from the adjectives which he habitually uses in conversation.

—MARK TWAIN

Good communication is just as stimulating as black coffee, and just as hard to sleep after.

—ANNE MORROW LINDBERGH

CALVIN IS A RATHER somber fellow, with neatly trimmed coal black hair, which he always, without exception, keeps parted on the right. He's the sort of orderly man who often pulls out his wallet just to check whether all his bills are facing in the same direction and, mind you, without any folded corners. His shoes have the air of being recently shined and, today, he's sitting at a round oak table in a French-owned coffee shop named, "La fontaine inattendue."[1] For the past fifteen minutes, Calvin has alternated between vigorously tapping his fingers on the oak surface, frowning at

1. "The unexpected Fountain"

his pocket watch, and adjusting the placement of his coffee, square napkin, pen and notepad, such that their locations on the table were all geometrically and logically pleasing to him. Calvin's impeccable posture permitted him the benefit of seeing his colleague B.F. approach the entrance of the coffee shop. Watching B.F. casually stroll into the coffee shop, with no look of hurriedness about him, Calvin muttered something to himself in French and abruptly returned his pocket watch to his jacket pocket.

Calvin: "Here you are late as usual, and it seems this time that Wesley has caught your disease!"

B.F.: "I do apologize Calvin . . . had a nap this afternoon and it persisted until quite recently. Rest's good for the mind you know."

Calvin: "You mean the brain," says Calvin with a grin, alluding to some prior discussion.

B.F.: "Yes, yes," acquiesces B.F. as he removes his plaid scarf and droops his pea coat over the back of the coffeehouse chair. "Well, according to me they are altogether the same thing; however, before you draw me into another meaningless squabble over synonyms, you should take note that it is Wesley and not me who is *latest* this round."

Calvin: "B.F., blaming your tardiness on *napping . . .*" Calvin pronounced this last word with such force and vigor, that some reserve saliva was obliged to exit his mouth and volley onto B.F.'s glasses," . . . will get you nowhere with me. You've known about this meeting and our topic for well beyond a week; for once take responsibility for yourself. It's only proper." Calvin folds his hands, slightly turns up his nose, and looks expectantly at his companion.

B.F.: "Indeed . . . propriety," responds B.F. sourly, grabbing Calvin's strategically-placed square napkin and wiping his glasses clean. "Remember your Shakespeare my friend '...for there is nothing either good or bad, but thinking makes it so.' Why then do you burden me with your preferences? Had you forgotten my victory in our last debate on ethical absolutes? I believe your tail was absolutely handed to you, if you'll permit me to summarize."

Calvin: Speaking seriously, "I think in your great exercise of rhetoric, B.F., you may have even persuaded yourself that winning a debate is the same as being right. They aren't and they never will be. It's one of Plato's great insights."

B.F.: "Yes . . . well," B.F. says smirking, "I am a bit more of an Aristotelian myself . . . and do you know, Calvin, what Lord Russell has said of the field of ethics?"

Calvin: "No, but I feel I may soon have the pleasure."

B.F.: "Yes, the old chap says quite insightfully, 'Ethics is the art of recommending to others what they must do to get along with ourselves.'" B.F. glances gaily at Calvin. "It follows my friend that you moral objectivists are quite universally difficult to placate."

Calvin: "And I suppose you would think it only *right* of me to acknowledge the truth of that statement?" Calvin demands, trying to catch B.F. with his words.

"Bling, Bling, Bling . . ." announces the bell attached to the entrance door of the coffeehouse. Wesley enters, disheveled, carrying some notes under his arm. He smiles warmly at his colleagues before sitting.

Wesley: "I hoped I'd never see the day that B.F. would be waiting on me. . . . I'm sorry if I have swayed you off course friends; what were you two old prigs discussing anyway?"

B.F.: Picking up this opportunity immediately, "Well, Calvin was just instructing me on the absolute irrelevance of argument and debate." B.F., now caught up in his own wit and cleverness, begins to smile from ear to ear as he waits for Wesley's response.

Wesley: "Our old Calvin lauding ignorance, I don't believe it!"

B.F.: "He does seem to fall back on that when he loses one."

Calvin: "Wesley, I'm afraid our friend may use his philosophical powers more to defend his taste than to decipher veracity, but nonetheless . . ." Calvin now returns a smile towards B.F. "I'll have nothing of these rabbit trails tonight and solely because this session's topic is so dear to me—the freedom of the will. I am simply overjoyed to hear both of your thoughts on this issue. I know, roughly, where you both stand now, and I'm sure you know where I stand as well, but won't it be interesting to see how we all think in a few days, or even the end of the night? A challenging conversation from friends does seem to carry this property in at least one possible world, namely, tending to produce genuine reflection. However . . ."

Calvin gazes proudly at his colleagues.

"I . . . I would like to say as well that I do appreciate being a part of this group. It is a rare thing indeed that one is able to regularly discuss the deeper things of life and reality with two friends, let alone two men of your intellectual caliber. And even though we often disagree, and sometimes ardently," he says with a nod towards B.F., "I do value our time here, very much so. So then, who would like to start us off? I think it is your turn, if I am not mistaken, B.F."

Dialogue 1

Whose Watch Is It Anyway?
Determinism Defended

When men strike for freedom, they strike against jails and the police, or the threat of them- against oppression. They never strike against forces which make them want to act the way they do.

— B.F. SKINNER, *WALDEN TWO*

Consider not only the consequences which flow from a given hypothesis, but the consequences which flow from denying the hypothesis.

— PARMENIDES, *THE DIALOGUES OF PLATO*

CALVIN'S EYES FELL UPON a tabletop menu as B.F. removed some papers from his jacket pocket. Near the top, facing him in decorative font, was the name of the coffeehouse:

Coffeehouse Compatibilism

La Fontaine Inattendue

Something in its placement, or style, or message reminded him of an announcement he had wished to share.

Calvin: "Pardon me, B.F., but before you start, I want to let you both know that one of my graduate students will be sitting in for our conversation tonight . . . . Wesley, I believe you have Rachel in your ethics course?"

Wesley: "Ah, yes, yes," he affirms, now cradling his cappuccino just below his chin, with the steam of it partially fogging his thick, brown-framed glasses.

Calvin: "She is studying this very issue in my metaphysics course and expressed that she hopes to gain some insight into, well… what types of implications the answer to this question may have for other areas of philosophy, such as ethics," he says with a nod towards Wesley, "or even religion."

B.F., who was not always very attentive when Calvin spoke, nor had he been traditionally much interested in the subject of religion, seemed very fascinated in Calvin's side of the coffee shop. Being so taken aback by the change, Calvin did a double-take. He realized that B.F. was looking past him, over his shoulder. Before Calvin could turn his head to see what the commotion was all about, B.F. precipitately began combing his moustache with a small, fine comb beckoned from— well— only God knows where. As a note of observation, B.F.'s moustache was similar, in the author's opinion, to an Olympic hurdle in three particular respects:

(1) its shape,

(2) the daunting feeling of forthcoming danger it gave a person, and

(3) the figurative manner in which one had to vault it to arrive at the rest of B.F.'s face.

"*Je suis désolée professeur, mais je pense que je suis un peu en retard.*"[1]

Calvin stands up, a bit surprised by her entrance.

Calvin: "*Non, je t'en prie,*" he articulates in his native tongue, "*assieds-toi là, s'il te plait.*"[2] While standing, he introduces Rachel to the other two men, "Wesley, I believe you and Rachel know each other."

Wesley: "Yes! good to see you outside of class, Rachel," he affirms, returning her grin and shaking her outstretched hand from across the table.

Rachel: "And you as well, professor. Professor Skinner, I don't believe we have had the pleasure of meeting yet, but I have heard many great things about you from your admiring students."

B.F.: "I have many admirers my dear . . . and yet I'd say I'm always recruiting." He smiles back at the young girl, whose face he finds curiously pleasant to gaze upon.

Calvin: "Well then," Calvin noisily interjects, "I see you have your notepad with you," he comments, motioning to Rachel. "If there is any point within our discussion where you are at a loss for the meaning of our terms or the specific logic of our arguments, please feel *free* to ask *at will.* I don't want you to feel *hindered* in any way," Calvin puns.

Wesley: Wesley, chuckling a bit to himself from Calvin's thoughtfully placed witticisms, adds, "yes, please feel a*t liberty to do as you please* throughout the evening, Rachel."

B.F., still taken more by Rachel's natural beauty and unpretentious demeanor than the humor of his friends, inquires, "So how is it that you have come to know French? Is this a part of your philosophical studies?"

Rachel: "Yes it is Professor Skinner. I actually spent a year studying the language in Noyon, which is a petite

1. "Excuse me professor, I think I'm a bit late."

2. "No worries, please have a seat."

Coffeehouse Compatibilism

city in northern France. It would be totally unknown to the world if it had not been the birthplace of a few great thinkers," Rachel artfully intimates, looking to Calvin to explain further.

Calvin: Nodding his head, noticeably delighted by her complaisance, he elaborates, "As chance would have it, Rachel happened to choose my home town to study in . . . . Yes, and I have asked her to converse in French with me when leisure allows, as it gives me great pleasure to speak in French outside the home. However, before you arrived, Rachel, B.F. was just getting ready to commence our dialogue this evening, so I will not hinder him any further."

B.F. opens some folded papers that he had lying on the table in front of him.

B.F.: "Knowing how much you theists like stories about watches, I thought I would begin our evening by speaking on the beautiful timepiece that we find ourselves in, or rather, a part of. The turning gears and integrated systems of our Newtonian world all spin to the melody of the mundane 'tic tic tic tic . . .' There are no autonomous oscillators, no maverick mechanisms, but each part is moved by its antecedent and moves its consequent in a magnificent parade of causation.[3] It will be my aim, therefore, this

3. See Elizabeth Anscombe, "Causality and Determinism" in Laura Waddell Ekstrom ed., *Agency and Responsibility*, (Westview press, 2001). Anscombe makes two interesting points herein, namely, one, that the laws of physics are too broad to "necessitate" a totally unique future, and, two, that there exist non-necessitating causes. These points are shown in the following two quotes respectively.

(1) "Newton's mechanics is a deterministic system; but this does not mean that believing them commits us to determinism. We could say: of course nothing violates those axioms or the laws of the force of gravity. But animals, for example, run about the world in all sorts of paths and no path is dictated for them by those laws, as it is for planets. Thus in relation to the solar system, the laws are like the

evening to buttress this conclusion, namely, that man is no more 'free' than a wooden top, which being flung out by some children, rolls this way and that."

B.F. pauses, glances towards Rachel, and recommences, "I suppose it would be fitting for me, in the presence of our guest, to quickly outline the main forms of determinism held today. There are four. First, physical determinism, which is essentially the type of thing I had just alluded to. It is the notion that, given the *determinant* way physical things interact, there is no room for freedom; unless of course you define it in the bizarre way Calvin does," B.F. banters. Calvin, seemingly accustomed to this sort of sarcasm, just continued sipping his coffee.

"So, on this thesis, the state of the physical world and the laws of nature entail a distinct future;[4] that is, given the way the world is at any moment, the laws of nature will carry the world in a fixed way and nothing can deviate from this path. So the two, the laws of nature and the state of the world, bring about all that is. They entail whether or not I will succeed at my greatest life goals, whether or not I will have any

---

rules of an infantile card game . . . once the cards are dealt the game is determined . . . But in relation to what happens on and inside a planet the laws are, rather, like the rules of chess; the play is seldom determined, though nobody breaks the rules." (p.68)

(2) "A non-necessitating cause is then one that can fail of its effect without the intervention of anything to frustrate it." (p. 69)

These two assertions aim to show that metaphysical determinism does not follow from an acceptance of Newton's laws. Given Newton's laws, it is still not clear that they are sufficiently narrow to allow for only one future outcome. If, as Anscombe puts it, these laws are more like the rules in a chess game, then they certainly do guide the result, but they also allow room for "other forces" to work.

4. Peter Van Inwagen, *An Essay on Free Will* (Oxford: Clarendon Press, 1985), 65.

9

goals, whether I will cheat on a test, cheat on my wife, and, in general, the state of every physical thing. As the great French determinist Laplace asserted, if one were able to know everything about the current moment and the laws by which the universe operates, one *could* predict the future,[5] and not only the next few moments, but the entirety of it."[6]

B.F., judging Rachel's face to see whether or not his explanations were sufficient, continues. "Rachel, did you ever play with dominoes when you were a child?"

Rachel: "Mmm . . . not really, but I know what they are. Why?"

B.F.: "Okay, well think of it like this. You have just set up ten dominoes in a sequence. You know the weight, height, and width of every piece. You know the distance between each piece and any external factors that may come into play in their toppling into each other, like the density of the air, the speed and direction of the breeze, et cetera. Now, if you could also know the exact force that was applied to the first member in sequence, you could easily devise an equation that could tell you when and with what momentum the

5. Daniel Dennett, *Elbow Room* (Cambridge: The MIT press, 1984), 51.

6. Robert Audi, ed., *The Cambridge Dictionary of Philosophy 2nd edition* (Cambridge University Press, 1999), 228–29. LaPlace also said that one could in principle retrodict the entirety of the past from the current moment and the laws of nature.

Karl Popper, "Indeterminism in Quantum physics and in Classical Physics, Part 1," *The British Journal for the Philosophy of Science*, Vol. 1, No. 2 (Aug. 1950), p. 122.

"The 'Laplacean demon' is a superhuman intelligence capable of knowing the positions, masses, and velocities of all elementary particles (point-masses) for a certain moment of time T^0. Laplace pointed out that this knowledge (we shall call it 'initial information') of the T^0 state of the world together with a knowledge of Newtonian theory of mechanics would enable the demon to predict, by way of logical or mathematical deduction, every future state of the world."

final piece would topple over. Now, take this idea and try and picture 1,000 dominoes or even 1,000 intersecting lines of 1,000 dominoes angling in different directions, each one pushing over the next.[7] This is the essential idea underlying[8] physical determinism."

Wesley: Wesley leans over to his right and says to Rachel, "*This* domino doesn't like being pushed around."

B.F.: "The second type, which is limited to the actions of people, or . . . at least, limited to beings with desires, is psychological determinism. As far as I can see, this bounded breed of determinism is normally coupled with some other form of overarching determinism. Whether this other form be physical or theological, it functions as a type of desire-engine. All the same, psychological determinism holds that we always act according to our greatest desire, and that our desires are placed into us by some 'desire-engine.' For instance, if the 'engine' is theological, then God implants desires into us either directly or indirectly; and if the engine is physical, then the physical word makes me desire the way I do. In either case, regardless of where these wants come from, I always follow them. My strongest desires *always* lead to action; that's psychological determinism.

The third and fourth varieties of determinism, theological and logical, are of analogous form; for theological determinism argues that because God knows the truth-value of some future-tense proposition,[9] then it *must* come to

7. The notion of physical determinism is much more complex than molecules bumping into each other. It encompasses forces such as gravity, the strong and weak nuclear forces, electromagnetism, et cetera. The main idea, however, is that there are some finite number of forces that can be known, in principle, and that, combined with the state of the world, lead to a distinct future.

8. For an event to be "determined," there must be, prior to that event, necessary and sufficient cause(s) for its occurrence.

9. "Knowing the truth-value of a proposition" is philosophical

pass. Likewise, logical determinism asserts that, regardless of whether anyone knows or not, a future-tense proposition has a truth-value before the event takes place; and, therefore, *must* occur in accord with this value."

Rachel: Rachel, brow furrowed and the end of her pen lightly tapping her notebook, interrupts, "Excuse me professor, but would you . . . elaborate a little more on theological and logical determinism?"

B.F.: "Certainly, my dear. Let's start with theological. So, throughout history, theologically-minded people have wondered how God's foreknowledge of everything, his omniscience, might affect free will. The problem goes along these lines: if God knows that tomorrow I will do X and God's foreknowledge is necessarily true, such that he *cannot* be wrong, then tomorrow I will *necessarily* do X. I must do X, for otherwise God would be wrong, which is impossible.[10] But, how can I be free if I have no genuine options, if I only do what I must do? Of course, this isn't a problem for those who don't have faith."

Wesley: "Nor for those who do."[11]

Calvin nods and Rachel studies Wesley's face, for there was passion in his voice.

B.F.: "Indeed . . ." B.F. replies, re-tracking his thoughts. "Yes, as I was saying Rachel, logical determinism is parallel

---

talk for "knows whether something is true or false."

10. "If God foreknows a thing, it necessarily happens (assuming that the scriptural position that God neither errs nor makes mistakes, is premised.) It would certainly be a hard question, I allow—indeed, an insoluble one—if you sought to establish both foreknowledge and the freedom of man together; for what is harder, yes, more impossible, than maintaining that contraries and contradictories do not clash?"

J. I. Packer & O. R. Johnston, translated. Martin Luther, *The Bondage of the Will* (Michigan: Fleming H. Revell, 1957), 215.

11. Cf. William Lane Craig, *The Only Wise God* & Alvin Plantinga, *Nature and Necessity*.

to this type of reasoning; however, it subtracts God. Their contention can be phrased in this way: if it is true right now that 'I will do X tomorrow' and no true propositions can be rendered false, then I will do X tomorrow. I am sure you have already noticed the resemblance between the two."

Rachel: "Yes, but logical determinism still seems a bit odd to me. What do you mean by 'one cannot render a proposition false'?"

B.F.: "Good question. Okay, let's look at an example proposition. Hmm . . . okay.

'The morning of April 21st, 2025, Calvin will get a tattoo.'"

Calvin smirks.

"So, this proposition must be true or false right now. Why is that so? Because that is one of the properties of propositions.[12] They are declarative sentences that make claims about reality, and because of that fact they must be true or false insofar as they accurately reflect what really is.[13] So, they have a truth-value and there are no middle states. It must be true *or* false. But, if this proposition is true after Calvin decides, it must also be true before he decides, because it was *always* a declarative statement about reality." B.F. notices that there is still some cloudiness for Rachel. "Another example . . . . Say, you were to check the weather before planning a picnic and the weatherman stated, 'Friday the 17th will be sunny and have an average temperature of 72 degrees.' Nonetheless, when Friday comes and it is cold and cloudy and you say to yourself, 'that weatherman

12. Peter Van Inwagen, *An Essay on Free Will* (Oxford: Clarendon Press, 1985), 58. Van Inwagen calls propositions "non-linguistic bearers of truth-value."

13. Ibid., 33. Quoting Aristotle, "To say of what is that it is not, or of what is not that it is, is false, while to say of what is that it is, and of what is not that it is not, is true."

was wrong, what he said wasn't true.' Do you see what I am getting at?"

Rachel: "Yeah, I think I understand now."

B.F.: "So the problem of logical determinism is that before Calvin is even born, all of the propositions concerning his life, such as the one we just said about him getting a tattoo, already have a truth-value. Consequently, if propositions like:

'Calvin will get married',

'Calvin will be a lying cheat',

and

'The morning of April 21st, 2025, Calvin will get a tattoo,'

already have a truth-value, what type of freedom could he have? It seems his story is already written, as it were. However, as I said before, I find physical determinism, coupled with the psychological aspect, the most attractive of the bunch. And that for . . ."

Wesley: "Attractive?!? I . . ."

B.F.: "Certainly, Wes. I say, you Libertarians don't have the market on beauty you know. Undeniably, the word 'freedom', straightaway, evokes sentiments of passion and credulity from the majority of people. But, there is an express type of beauty in the fixed, mechanical manner in which our universe operates. As a matter of fact, you referenced this very type of thing when we were discussing the intelligent design arguments a few weeks back. It was for this very reason I used the watch analogy to begin tonight. It seems to me, regardless of whether or not the watchmaker is blind, we all agree we have something elegant before us."

"Moreover," he pauses, "although I was going to save this for later, I would like to read a small section from Lord Russell's work to illustrate that there is a type of beauty in accepting our place in this world.

That man is the product of causes which had no
prevision of the end they were achieving; that
his origin, his growth, his hopes and fears, his
loves and his beliefs, are but the outcome of ac-
cidental collocations of atoms; that no fire, no
heroism, no intensity of thought and feeling,
can preserve an individual life beyond the grave;
that all the labours of the ages, all the devotion,
all the inspiration, all the noonday brightness of
human genius, are destined to extinction in the
vast death of the solar system, and that the whole
temple of Man's achievement must inevitably
be buried beneath the debris of a universe in
ruins—all these things, if not quite beyond dis-
pute, are yet so nearly certain, that no philosophy which rejects them can hope to stand. Only
within the scaffolding of these truths, only on
the firm foundation of unyielding despair, can
the soul's habitation henceforth be safely built . . .
But the *beauty* of Tragedy does but make visible
a quality which, in more or less obvious shapes,
is present always and everywhere in life.

Wesley: "Isn't this quote taken from *A Free Man's Wor-
ship*?" he responds, noticeably putting emphasis on 'free.'

Calvin: Before B.F. can respond to Wesley's joke, Calvin counsels, "Gentlemen, I think this may be getting us
a bit off subject. Surely the aesthetics of determinism play
little to no role in our acceptance of it."

B.F.: "Well said, Calvin. The aesthetic appeal of determinism is not, in itself, a reason I have for maintaining
the doctrine; however, if I may, it is something that I have
gained a taste for over the years. No, my reasons for holding
to determinism are twofold. Primarily, I think it goes well
with our scientific knowledge. No, I want to say more than
this. The scientific endeavor assumes it! I mean, what would
scientists do if they did not have the guiding principle of

determinism for their work? Isn't it their sole business to search for causes? And what would the world be like if events had no sufficient causes? Water would freeze, sometimes at thirty-two degrees Fahrenheit and at other times at fifty-seven. Physics would be impossible. Moreover, it seems that even our language assumes determinism, for words like 'because,' 'since,' and 'as a result of' would have no meaning if events did not have sufficient causes."

B.F. stops and looks down at the table.

"Of course I am being a bit facetious here; for I know Wesley, that you do not deny that there exist sufficient causes, but I want to stress the importance and centrality of them for science. If scientists generally believed that finding causes was a rare circumstance, they would have little reason to look for them and the enterprise of science would collapse. This is why the metaphysical doctrine of determinism, that there always exist sufficient causes for events, must be assumed. Thus, seeing as we all have reason to accept the scientific endeavor, with all of her successes for our practical lives, we all have reason as well to accept determinism, her guiding principle. Secondly, I see no *good* reasons for positing that we are agent-substances as Wesley wants to argue; and as far as your hybrid Calvin, well…with all due respect, I think the adage 'you can't have your cake and eat it too' could be applied to your notion of moral responsibility within a deterministic framework."

Wesley: "May I interject something here, B.F.?"

B.F.: "Please."

Wesley: "Both the way you stressed sufficient causes and your earlier comment about the Laplacean demon lead me to ask this: but how do you see quantum physics affecting free will and someone's ability to tell the future? For instance, taking off of your earlier analogy, the Heisenberg uncertainty principle would seem to make it impossible to know both the position and speed of all the dominoes."

B.F.: "Yes, this is true and I should have said more on this in my introduction; however, I believe many scientists are hopeful that it will soon be replaced by a broader, more uniform theory. And as I see it, it doesn't change much for our discussion on free will. Don't get me wrong. Quantum mechanics is all well and good, but the amount of impact it makes in any large level experiments, let alone human decisions, seems miniscule. It may temper ideas of precise prediction of the location and speed of quarks, but on the macro-level, most of the dominoes are tumbling as normal. I guess you could say it is the difference between determined and *determined for all practical purposes*.[14] And besides, a quantum blip or a maverick electron doesn't seem like the sort of thing that would bestow free will on a man anyhow."

Wesley: "You are right about that . . ."

Rachel: "But I thought that the falsity of determinism was what libertarians were arguing for?"

Wesley: Wesley looks to B.F. before answering, not wanting to interrupt his response. "No. Not exactly. What libertarians are looking for is to put the agent *in control* of her actions. It may be the case that scientists end up finding no replacement theory to subsume the indeterminacy of quantum physics. If this is the case, then many events in our world will prove to be undetermined, that is, they could have happened differently than they did given our past. However, this being the case, it still wouldn't be true that the agent is in control of her actions in such a world . . . . Although I know some Libertarians who believe that quantum physics does much in the area of offering a platform on which to base our conception of free will, I find their ideas mistaken. To me,

14. Peter Van Inwagen, *An Essay on Free Will* (Oxford: Clarendon Press, 1985), 197–98.

the only clear method to maintain *Libertarian* freedom is through the means of an agent substance." Then he teases, "But, doubtlessly, all this rests on the assumption that Libertarian freedom proves to be something *worth wanting*."[15]

B.F.: "I am right there with you, Wes. Albeit I am not a Libertarian, but it appears to me as well that event-causal libertarianism is sorely mistaken about claiming the agent controls their decisions.[16] If all of my desires and actions are nondeterministically caused by uncaused, random events, I don't see how that gives me control[17] and certainly not enough control to be morally responsible."

15. Daniel Dennett, *Elbow Room* (Cambridge: The MIT press, 1984), 153.

"The varieties of free will we deem worth wanting are those—if there are any-that will secure for us our dignity and responsibility. If, inspired by some philosophical analysis, we develop a yearning for 'contra-causal freedom' or the capacity to exhibit 'agent causation,' for instance, it is because we have been convinced by that analysis rightly or wrongly that just such a metaphysical blessing is a necessary condition for the sort of free will that any responsible, dignified, moral agent must have."

16. Robert Kane, John Martin Fischer, Derk Pereboom, Manuel Vargas, *Four Views on Free Will*, (Blackwell, 2007), 102–3. "There are two major versions of libertarianism, the event-causal and the agent-causal types. In event-causal libertarianism, actions are caused solely by way of states or events, and some type of indeterminacy in the production of actions by appropriate states or events is held to be a decisive requirement for moral responsibility . . . On an event-causal libertarian theory, with the causal role of these antecedent conditions already given . . . There is nothing else about [the agent] that can settle whether the decision to stop occurs, since in this view her role in producing a decision is exhausted by antecedent states or events in which she is involved . . . there is no provision that allows the agent to have control over whether the decision occurs or not . . ."

I personally find this objection to event-causal libertarianism, given by Derk Pereboom, very convincing.

17. Randolph Clarke, "Toward a credible agent-causal account of Free Will" in Gary Watson ed., *Free Will*, (Oxford: University press,

Wesley: ". . . I have another comment for you B.F. I am not stealing the floor, am I Calvin?"

Calvin: "Oh, certainly not."

Wesley: "Ok, well. It is curious, B.F., that you came from quoting Russell's essay, because something in that essay, and in a consonant passage from your friend Mr. Dennett's work, have puzzled me. Could I read them for us?"

B.F., who had been leaning back with his legs crossed, changed positions and leans forward with concern. He had been meeting Wesley long enough to realize when he was going to say something profound.

B.F.: "Please do."

Wesley: "Ok, first Russell:

> A strange mystery it is that Nature, omnipotent but blind, in the revolutions of her secular hurryings through the abysses of space, has brought forth at last a child, subject still to her power, but gifted with sight, with knowledge of good and evil, with the capacity of judging all the works of his unthinking Mother.

And now Mr. Dennett:

> I can never decide whether this is a tragic or comic vision: the deterministic world unfolds over the eons, eventually producing creatures who gradually grow in rationality and curiosity to the fatal point where they can be caused, inexorably...to see the futility of their frantic, scheming ways.'[18]

2003), 287. ". . . it is unclear how the agent could be related to [an] uncaused event in such a way that she controlled its occurrence, and by controlling its occurrence determined which action she should perform."

18. Daniel Dennett, *Elbow Room* (Cambridge: The MIT press, 1984), 104.

So, there it is. The intriguing, and terribly peculiar notion, that we not only are determined, but *we happen to know it*. I am sure the both of you have already wrestled through the queerness of it, but for me, it is striking."

B.F.: "I think you should say more, Wesley. I am not sure I follow you."

Wesley places his glasses on the table.

Wesley: "Well, I guess I am just expressing that it seems bizarre to me. Bizarre that we humans, likely the only intelligent life this universe has ever churned out,[19] happened also to be determined to discover our dilemma, to discover our . . . chains."

His laser focus centered on B.F.

". . . And I don't think the peculiarity of it can be explained away, as Dennett intimates, by saying that we humans can reason and so, certainly . . . we would have eventually figured it out. Since we can think, deliberate, and deduce, since, as a type of self-tamed animal, we have discovered mathematics, perfected the sciences, and created medicine, surely, Dennett would say, we have the ability to conclude that we are determined. No, I believe this is mistaken, for our reasoning processes, if metaphysical determinism obtains,[20] are determined as well. So, what good is it to say that we have an ability, like reasoning, if the use of that ability is switched on and off by another. No, the peculiarity sticks. From moment one, from the hatching egg of the Big Bang's gravitational singularity, we were meant to discover it."

19. Cf. Peter Ward & Donald Brownlee, *Rare Earth: Why Complex Life is Uncommon in the Universe* (New York: Copernicus books, 2000).

20. Philosophers often use the word 'obtains' to mean "is true and actual in this world."

Calvin: "I'm not sure I understand what you are saying. What is 'it'?"

Wesley: "Think of it in terms of the story of Pinocchio." He smiles, looks at Rachel, and says, "I actually thought of this on my way here . . . . Do you like analogies, Rachel?"

Rachel: "Particularly, yes."

Wesley: "Good. Okay, the woodcarver Geppetto, which in our version can represent blind, dumb, Mother Nature, crafts Pinocchio, gives him the desire to be a real boy and then turns his little puppet head and makes him look into the mirror . . . forces him to see the strings on his arms and the paint on his face. Geppetto forces him to see what he really is. It's sinister, isn't it? And that's the story in which we are all characters. So . . . in the words of Russell, 'our unthinking mother' who bore us and who sang to us the freedom lullabies of the Republic while we nursed at her breast has now, in our adulthood, leaked the secret that she's been sweethearts with the monarch."

Eyes glazed over, Calvin's mouth rests open as he taps the tip of his chin and looks into the distance. Rachel meticulously observes each professor in turn, and B.F. rechecks his empty mug for more.

B.F.: ". . . I had never thought of it like that," B.F. mutters to himself.

Calvin: "Wow, what are the chances?" Calvin shot out, sarcastically.

Wesley: "I wish I knew. In my estimation, though, they are slim. For those who recognize the extreme improbability of generating intelligent life from nothing, the added doubtfulness of this new addendum is too much." Wesley's eyes are wide open and he shakes his head in incredulity.

Rachel: "What addendum professor?"

Wesley: "That of all the propositions we were fated to uncover, of all the random lists of claims that the universe could have marked down for our future epistemic inventory. We're stuck with this one. I find it all a tad ironic."

Everyone rested silent for a few moments before Calvin cleared his throat.

Calvin: "I also have a comment, B.F. You mentioned that the enterprise of science depends on the doctrine of metaphysical determinism. This seems misconstrued. Couldn't science get along just fine without any metaphysical doctrines?"

B.F.: "I think not. Science *is* metaphysical determinism. If scientists did not have this guiding principle in their work, they wouldn't search for causes, and . . ."

Calvin: "Wait a second, B.F. I think you are confusing the Principle of Universal Causation[21] with metaphysical determinism here, because earlier you agreed with Wesley that uncaused, random, quantum events can cause other events."

B.F. leans back into his chair, partially shocked by his blunder.

Calvin: "Moreover, although this is beside the point, it doesn't even seem clear that science depends on the Principle of Universal Causation for it to function. Yeah, I mean,

'There may be some events that do not have discernible causes, or any causes at all, but look anyway,'[22]

could function as a guiding maxim for the scientific community."[23]

---

21. Peter Van Inwagen, *An Essay on Free Will* (Oxford: Clarendon Press, 1985), 3. "Determinism . . . must be carefully distinguished from what we might call the Principle of Universal Causation, that is, from the thesis that every event . . . has a cause."

22. Or, regardless of the aforementioned fact, continue doing science.

23. For a fuller argument on this topic see: Kai Nielsen, "Is to abandon determinism to withdraw from the enterprise of science?" *Philosophy and Phenomenological Research*, Vol. 28, No. 1 (Sept.1967), p.117–21.

Wesley: "I'm not so sure about that Calvin, for they may be a bit less enthusiastic to search if there were a possibility that they wouldn't find anything, but you were certainly right about the whole metaphysical determinism bit. I was going to ask about that earlier. . . . Likewise, and I guess this next question would apply to both of you, so either one of you can feel free to take a shot at it. What are your thoughts on the problem determinism presents for deliberation?"

Calvin: "What problem?"

Wesley: "Well, let's see. Should I tell you the argument that I concluded upon by my rational faculties or the one that I was led to have through the direct and unbroken causal influences of those irrational, non-teleologically-minded quarks?"

Calvin: "Ahh . . . I see." Calvin's forehead was as wrinkled as ever; and yet B.F.'s face lacked expression.

Wesley: "The problem is: how does reason get its hold on the brain? In the case that our psychological life, encompassing our choices and rationality, is fundamentally just the music being drummed out by the material world then any argument for determinism would seem to supply its own defeater.[24] If your argument for determinism undermines our reasons to trust human rationality, and thus the rationality of your very argument, then so much the worse for your argument. We're keeping reason!"

Wesley chuckles, feeling he has the upper hand.

"So, we seem to find ourselves at a crossroads. Assuming that your arguments for determinism can be shown

24. "A defeater removes or weakens justification for belief... [undercutting defeaters] do not directly attack the thing believed (by trying to show that it is false), but rather they attack the notion that R is a good reason for Q."

J.P. Moreland & William Lane Craig, *Philosophical Foundations for a Christian Worldview*, (Downers Grove: Intervarsity Press, 2003), 88.

false, obviously we would have no reason to consent to your thesis. On the other hand, even if your arguments *seem* to follow logically, because they have the *untenable entailment* that your logic is the result of physics and not unhindered Socratic pondering, we again have no reason to accept determinism. So, no matter how you slice it, you find yourself on the horns of one nasty dilemma." Wesley continues mercilessly, as a hound dog in mid-chase, "In fact, your argument suffers the same fate as that of Mr. Dorian Gray who, upon stabbing the grisly image in the mural found the twisted blade in his own chest . . ."

Wesley's discourse is disturbed by the ringing of his own portable phone. He looks at the caller-id and winks at Calvin.

"Oh-ho, saved by the bell, as it were . . . . I must take this call, please carry on without me," he apologizes, pulling his Chicago Bears jacket off of the back-support of his chair, where it had been draped thirty minutes before.

Calvin: Calvin stands up too. "And as for me, I'm taking a restroom break."

Rachel finds herself at the table, alone, with Professor Skinner. She notices him across the table, noticing her.

Rachel: To break the silence, she starts, "Professor Skinner . . ."

B.F.: ". . . please call me B.F. That's what my friends call me," he says, in a pitch slightly lower than moments before.

Rachel: Rachel, blushing a bit, tries to turn the focus to philosophy, "Yes, thank you . . . B.F., what do you think of the issue that Wesley raised?"

B.F.: "I feel the weight of his argument; however, if metaphysical determinism were true, it is difficult to see how an argument like his would make any difference . . . . What I mean to say is that his argument isn't against the possibility that determinism, as previously defined, is true.

Yes, the interesting thing about Wes' argument, the peculiar thing that it is, is that it is actually against the rationality of us accepting determinism and not against determinism *qua* determinism."

Rachel: "How do you mean?"

B.F.: "Wes's argument is: 'it is irrational for us to believe determinism because X.' Not 'determinism is false because X.' These are two different claims. Do you understand?"

Rachel: "Yes, I see. Obviously I will need to do some more thinking on it, but I comprehend the general idea. And, his earlier comment about the unlikelihood of determinism, what do you make of that?"

B.F.: "I found it brilliant! I had a similar analogy I was ready to share tonight to illustrate the impact of the question of determinism on morality, dignity, et cetera and it parallels Wes' in many respects. After these weekly debates with Wes, I find myself talking more and more in stories and analogies. Ok, so picture humanity, if you will, as Dorothy from the *Wizard of Oz*. Throughout the history of our miserable existence in Oz, we have been fighting the Wicked Witch and her evil flying monkeys…well to be frank, I hadn't thought of a way I could incorporate them," he jests. "Regardless, whether flying monkeys or taunting trees, we are fighting the problem of evil in all its excess as we bumble over one yellow brick at a time. We sing and make light of our sufferings all the while hoping to find fulfillment, hoping to find answers in the Emerald City. However, after this long passage, after all our dancing and prayers, when we pull back the curtain we find a deaf and dumb monster banging his hands indiscriminately on the master console of our lives. We came to find healing, to receive a heart. And what befell us? We lost hope, hope that there was someone, *an agent*, in the Emerald City. Hope that the "evil" of the witch would be punished. How does that affect deontological ethics? What implications does it have for human rights and the idea of a human nature? It destroys them. Where do we go from here, Rachel?" B.F., now utterly sober, looks her in the eyes and says, "Deaf, dumb, DNA is calling the shots and as Wes said 'we know it.'"

Calvin: Calvin returns with food. "My stomach is *calling the shots* tonight," he mutters. "These macadamia nut cookies are seriously addictive."

Rachel was thinking to herself that she was glad she had come tonight. She had never seen Calvin act so casually. And she had the sneaking suspicion that she was going to walk away from this discussion with more real understanding than a month's worth of reading could accomplish.

Wesley returns to the table.

Wesley: "Sorry about that, everyone. It was my brother Charles calling from London."

Calvin: "All's well I presume."

Wesley: "Yes, nothing serious. Just some news from Parish, but seeing as we don't speak much, I thought I should take the call. Well, I hate to give up an occasion to re-press my argument, but I am afraid we must be moving along if we are ever to finish before they kick us out; and the honor is Calvin's, I believe."

The three heads turn to Calvin who, as it happens, is enjoying the last bite of what had been a Frisbee sized cookie.

Calvin: "*Bon* . . . uh, good. I'm ready," he responds amidst the smacking and licking of his lips, still savoring the lingering sweetness.

B.F.: "I would still like to give my closing statement… for Rachel's benefit," B.F. said.

Wesley: "Oh, certainly. Wrap it all up."

B.F.: "Okay. The large and small of it, my dear, is that our world, being the way it is, does not leave us with the type of freedom necessary for ethical responsibilities. If determinism is true, and there is no immaterial agent to step outside the system of causation, as Wes will speak to us about later, then we are all stuck marching in the same parade. However, it can be a freeing discovery if you let it. I will leave you with this thought: what would life be like if you knew that you could not be judged and neither you, nor anyone else for that matter, had any right to judge others. Ideas like retributive justice and their ilk would find no place in our minds or societies. We would realize that we are like a child on the back of an elephant and wherever it takes us is where we go. We have no power. We have only our passions to guide us. We have only our desires to live for. There is no 'good and evil,' there is only the mere unfolding of the given."[25]

Calvin fumbled through his notes, and realized that he had left his talking points in the car.

Calvin: As he stands, he explains, "I seem to have left my outline in the car. Let's have a break. Rachel, you can get yourself a beverage if you like."

25. Robert Kane, John Martin Fischer, Derk Pereboom, Manuel Vargas, *Four Views on Free Will*, (Blackwell, 2007), 67. This quotation, "mere unfolding of the given" is quoted by John Fischer from Saul Smilansky. See also: Saul Smilansky, *Free Will and Illusion*, (Oxford: Clarendon Press, 2000).

Further Reading: Hard Incompatibilist / Determinist

Derk Pereboom: *Living Without Free Will* (Cambridge: Cambridge University Press, 2001)

Ted Honderich: *How Free Are You?* (Oxford: Oxford University Press, 2002)

Dialogue 2

Compatible or Intractable?

Nowadays, we have a soft determinism which abhors harsh words, and repudiating fatality, necessity and even predetermination, says that its real name is 'freedom.'

—WILLIAM JAMES, *THE DILEMMA OF DETERMINISM*

On your analysis, persons can *jump the fence even though their doing so here and now is impossible, given the past and the laws of nature. That is not what we libertarians mean by 'can'. . .*

—ROBERT KANE, *FOUR VIEWS ON FREE WILL*

PROFITING FROM THE BREAK, Rachel visited the ladies' room and now approaches the lit glass display where the delicacies of the café wait to be admired and purchased. Laughter and dialogue hum in the backdrop, giving place every so often to the sounds of the espresso machine and the clinking of glass mugs. Rachel applies a fresh coat of lip gloss and rolls her lips slowly one over the other, throwing her head forward as she checks her makeup in a small mirror.

A young man grins and advances. "What'll ya have miss?"

Rachel: "Espresso, please."

By the time she has the money out of her pocket, the drink is waiting in front of her.

"Thank you kindly."

As Rachel returned to the table, she found the professors in humorous commotion.

B.F.: "And would you like to know Calvin's life motto?!" he asked, trying to speak over the laugher. "Anything you can do I can do *meta*. I can do anything meta than you!"[1]

Wesley nearly spits out his coffee and begins to chuckle. Calvin, cool and phlegmatic as he is, holds a stolid expression except for one eyebrow sarcastically curled.

Calvin: Calvin begins to speak, notices Rachel has returned to her chair, and banters, "You say 'Tom-ay-to' and I say 'Tom-ah-to.' You see a chair and I see a substance with properties like four-legged-ness." Calvin shrugs his shoulders *as if* to ask, "What's a guy to do?"

B.F.: "You know, Calvin, just now your ridiculous babble about substances has called to mind how much I detest your friend, Professor Rousseau."

Calvin: "I can't see how. He's a very caring man."

Wesley: "Professor Rousseau?"

B.F.: "Yes, yes, he is the professor of French literature and culture. Only he loves to push his nose into the world of political philosophy. I cannot tell you how many of my students ask to write about the innate goodness of man, the evils of property ownership, and various other fatuities."

Wesley: "Teaching the evils of property ownership in America? What scandal! He may cause a revolution."

Calvin: "So, just because he is French you think we are friends?" Calvin questions incredulously.

---

1. Naturalists often tease metaphysicians about always making issues into ones fundamentally about metaphysical realities.

B.F.: "Honestly, it was because he speaks nonsense that I thought you were friends."

Cradling her espresso cup with both hands in front of her face, Rachel's sipping made a slight slurp that momentarily disrupted the injuries.

Calvin: Finding common ground, Calvin accommodates, "I've never really agreed with Rousseau's anthropology. It seems clear to me that we're all a bunch of rats . . . some more than others."

B.F. smiles broadly, knowing that Calvin was referring to him and enjoying every joust of the dialogue.

Calvin: "However, we should get back on key. My talk shall be based upon 5 points, which I believe hold together in logical unity and are representative of my whole philosophy on this topic. I shall delineate the points as follows:

(1) *T*esting our definitions

(2) *U*nderstanding the Conditional Analysis

(3) *L*imits of the thesis of alternate possibilities

(4) *I*nto the deep self

(5) *P*etition for the preservation of ethics

First, testing our definitions . . ."

Calvin looks to Rachel and asks rhetorically, "Rachel, do you know the three most important words in the real estate business? Location, location, location. As I am sure you have come to learn, it is not much different in philosophy. When one wants to develop one's thinking, one must pay close attention to one's definitions. That's why my first lesson in my metaphysics course each year is called, 'Definitions, Definitions, Definitions.' In fact, Compatibilism, which is the view that I will be supporting tonight, is a viewpoint birthed out of this very notion. When the libertarians and hard incompatibilists[2] were arguing about the question of freedom, we compatilists came along and solved their quarrel with just a clarification of definition. Consider these two propositions:

(Q) Every event/action has a sufficient cause

(R) All my actions are free[3]

It is certainly not clear that these two propositions are in conflict. They are at least not what philosophers would call *explicitly* contradictory. Yet, these are the two propositions over which the incompatibilists, like Wesley and B.F., have been squabbling. Wesley wants to say that (R) is certain and, thus, we should question the validity of (Q). B.F., on the other hand, finds it prima facie more plausible to accept (Q) and call into doubt (R). All of this is done because they both believe a third premise; a premise that neither one of them has stated or argued for. This third premise may not even be known to them, but it guides their reasoning to this conclusion.

This third tacit proposition may look like the following," Calvin says scribbling some symbols on the back on his sheet of notes.

$$Q \mathbin{\&} R \to {\sim}S, \ Q \mathbin{\&} S \to {\sim}R, \ R \mathbin{\&} S \ {\sim}Q$$

2. (Read: determinists).

3. Libertarian Robert Kane makes an important point on this account. Libertarians do not require that all of their actions be free (or equally free), but only that at least at some point in their lives the agent acted freely and that these free actions formed the character that the current actions flow out of. Said differently, if I am responsible for action X, which may be fully explainable by my character, then there must exist some actions in my past life that, while forming my character, found their sufficient cause in me. See also Robert Kane, John Martin Fischer, Derk Pereboom, Manuel Vargas, *Four Views on Free Will*, (Blackwell, 2007), 13–22.

He begins again,

"(S) All events/actions with sufficient causes are not events/actions that can be rightly called 'free'

However, we must realize that clandestine propositions such as these obfuscate our logic. If (S) is at stake, let us argue about (S) and not speak as if (Q) and (R) are the deciding factors. What I believe has happened is that the incompatibilists have built (S) into their definition of freedom. They have said, both Wesley and B.F., that to be free is not to have any sufficient causes for one's actions. But why should we define freedom like that? Why not rather define freedom in some other way? Take for instance, this definition: a person is free to the extent that she is able to do or get what she wants.[4]

Yes, it's clear that this argument about free will must be settled not by denying statements (Q) or (R), but by denying (S). In my humble opinion, we have wasted much time debating which of the two patently obvious premises above (Q & R) is false, when we should have been debating the unspoken proposition that made us think we had to make such a decision. We must spend the needed time combing through our definition of freedom to get to rid ourselves of the scraggly hairs that do not belong. We must look at (S). "

Wesley: "Not that I am agreeing with you Calvin, but weren't we speaking about this precise thing in relation to the problem of evil a few months back? If my memory serves me right, you had made a similar point."

Calvin: "Right indeed. Let me think. We were speaking about how many atheologians give the following propositions as an argument against the existence of God.

---

4. Gary Watson, "Free Agency" in Gary Watson ed., *Free Will*, (Oxford: University press, 2003), 337. This is an exact quotation of Watson's words taken from his introduction.

1. God is omnipotent

2. God is omniscient

3. God is wholly good

4. Evil exists

The propositions are supposed to give the hearer the impression that either evil does not exist, or God does not, or that God exists but without one of these properties (i.e. all-powerful, all-knowing, all-good). However, this dilemma is the entailment of these propositions (1-4) added with that of an unstated proposition (5). The atheologians never properly state this extra premise, but it is always there, waiting in secret to be caught by a watchful eye.[5]

Therefore, the atheologians' argument works much like that of the incompatibilists' argument. They present what at first appears like an insurmountable predicament through a few propositions. They then proceed to impress the weight of some added proposition, usually through rhetoric and sophistry, upon the listener until the listener feels the weight of their argument. Since they have concealed their weakest premise from you, you are unable to call it into question. All that they have revealed are the strong propositions . . . . Nevertheless, I don't want to steer us back into that conversation, but I just wanted to make this point clear. Many times there are tacit premises in an argument or what I like to call 'loaded-definitions.' When we pull these premises out into the open, we find that, not only were they bearing the load of the argument, but they are not at all plausible once we look at them for what they are. Is that clear enough?"

Rachel nods hesitantly.

5. See Alvin Plantinga, *God, Freedom, and Evil*, (Grand Rapids: Eerdman's, 1977) A candidate for (5) might be: (5) A good being eliminates every evil that it knows about and that it can eliminate.

"Perfect. So, before I move onward to my second main point, I would like to make a few clarifying remarks. There are many Compatibilists that are not determinists. Being a Compatibilist does not tie you to any particular view on the subject of determinism. I find that this is often confused. De facto, Compatibilists largely hold that the difference between free and un-free actions has nothing to do with the truth or falsity of determinism.[6] Also, there are many disparate types of Compatibilists as there are many types of Determinists and Incompatibilists. We must keep this in mind as we progress."

Wesley: "Well said, Calvin." Wesley, now gazing over at Rachel, counsels in fatherly admonition, "We must never make the assumption that we understand before we've listened. A wise person once said, 'We should be quick to listen and slow to speak and slow to become angry.'"

Calvin : "I am happy to hear you say that Wes . . . . Okay, let's move on now to the Conditional Analysis of freedom. True freedom can be, and certainly has been, defined in a plethora of ways throughout history. It is my opinion that these disparate definitions all have some common themes, namely, (1) freedom is controlling our actions, (2) freedom is having alternatives, and (3) freedom is doing what we desire without *external* compulsion. Compatibilists resonate with these truths and have created an analysis of freedom that can make sense of all of them, while, at the same time, not obliging us to know from our arm-chairs whether the scientific thesis of determinism is true or false. This analysis is called, very appropriately, the conditional analysis. Let me explain it to you by example. One might say that the following proposition is true under the conditional analysis framework, 'Today, B.F. would have ordered a soda had he

6. Gary Watson, "Free Agency" in Gary Watson ed., *Free Will*, (Oxford: University press, 2003), 338.

wanted to, but he ordered a coffee.' This seems very plausible and innocuous. B.F. was in control of his actions, he did exactly what he desired to do, and in a sense he had alternatives. Had he wanted to do otherwise, he would have done otherwise. This is what puts the 'conditional' in 'conditional analysis.' 'If he had wanted X, he would have done X.' I can't see how anyone could want more freedom than that, always doing what you want."

Wesley: "Pardon me, Calvin, but when you say 'he had alternatives,' what do you mean by that?"

Calvin: "What I mean by 'he had alternatives,' is that had B.F. wanted to order a soda, he would have ordered a soda, but he did not want that. He wanted coffee, so he ordered coffee. There was nothing external to B.F. that forced him to choose coffee; he did that because that's what he wanted. If I had twisted his arm to make him order it, or if I had shocked him with a Taser every time he thought of another beverage, I could see questioning his freedom in that act. But as it was, B.F. was not compelled by any external source to order coffee. He just wanted coffee and got it."

Wesley: Wesley presses his point further, "Yes, I understand that B.F. wanted coffee and chose coffee. And I also understand that had B.F. wanted soda, or anything else for that matter, he would have chosen that. But could he have wanted soda? Could he, at that very moment in time, have wanted anything other than coffee?"

Calvin: Perplexed by the direction of Wes' question, begins, "I suppose . . ."

Wesley: Wesley clarifies, "Think of it this way Calvin. Compatibilists define freedom by the conditional analysis. My understanding of this analysis is to say that, fundamentally, 'If a person wants X, that person will do X.' This is freedom. If I want to pick up this napkin, I will pick up this napkin, barring something prevents me. So, the conditional analysis leads me to believe that doing as I desire is true freedom. If we do what we want to do, then we are free. Am I right in this synopsis?"

Calvin: "Perfectly."

Wesley: "Well then. I ask you again, could B.F. have wanted anything other than coffee at that very moment in time when he was ordering?"

B.F.: Before Calvin could answer, B.F. chimes in, carrying Wes' argument forward a few steps. "No, I could not have. For if determinism is true, as I believe it is, and as Calvin wishes to allow for, I could not have wanted anything different from what I indeed did want at that moment in time. My desire for coffee was the inexorable outcome of the events of the remote past and the laws of nature working upon them. Coffee was . . . ," B.F. grins at Rachel, "my destiny this evening."

Calvin: "I don't see why we need to bring determinism back into this conversation. I'm talking about doing as we please, about acting on our desires . . ."

Wesley: "Yes, of course, Calvin. But you need to realize something here. What difference does it make to say that I do what I want if my wants are determined?"

Calvin, now feeling the sting of this pointed and insightful objection, just leans back in his chair, puffs out his lips, and begins nervously tapping his chin with his forefinger.

Wesley: Wes continues, now more in a mode of clarification for Rachel than for Calvin, "If we consider freedom as doing what we want, we must consider where our wants come from. If determinism is true and all of our desires are consequences of things outside our control, then we really aren't any more responsible for them than a computer is for the software it runs. No, freedom is found in real undetermined choices, in alternate possibilities."

Calvin: Seeking to salvage, or even gain the upper hand, Calvin throws out, "I'm not so sure about that, Wes. Adding alternate possibilities to the mix adds nothing. I know you'll give your own positive definitions and arguments later, but I'm assuming you would define freedom as, 'the ability to do otherwise.' Am I correct?"

Wesley: "Roughly."

Calvin: "Ok, moving from this assumption, if I can show you a situation in which a person did not have the ability to do otherwise, then you would have to say they did not have freedom." Calvin leans forward now, and raises his eyebrows, as if to gain permission to advance.

Rachel: Rachel, mouth agape, raises her pen in the air, signifying she'd like to interject. "Pardon me, professor. Could you please explain the difference in the way you define freedom from the way Wesley defines it?"

Calvin: "Certainly, my dear. My position is that a past action was free if the person would have done otherwise, had he or she wanted to do otherwise. This is essentially the same thing as saying that if the person was not externally coerced to do the action, but chose the action of their own will and for their own reasons, he or she made a free decision.

The upside of my definition of freedom is that one need not know whether or not the thesis of determinism is true. Wes' position, on the other hand, is that true freedom requires alternate possibilities or, said differently, that alternate courses of action be genuinely available to us. I would guess he'd say that doing what we want is not free enough. We must be able to do otherwise, which, if determinism is true, would be impossible. So again, for me freedom is doing what we want. Wherever the desires come from, whatever influences act upon us, at the end of the day, we are responsible for what we want and do."

Rachel: "Thank you, professor. I think I get it now."

Calvin: "Good questions, Rachel. Ok, so where was I . . . ?"

Wesley: "You were about to give an example in which one can be free without there existing alternate possibilities for that person. So, the person was free even though she could not have acted in any other way than the way she did act."

Calvin: "Ah, yes. Ok. So, picture this. Dr. Nefarious, a brilliant and resourceful – and devilishly greedy - neuroscientist opens a hotdog stand in downtown New York City. Be assured, this is no everyday hotdog stand. No, this hotdog stand emits radio signals on such a frequency and at such a voltage that it can control people's minds within a three-foot radius. At first, Dr. Nefarious performed only rather harmless actions with his mind-controlling-bratwurst-brain-ray, such as having every customer put extra onion on their hotdog or having them squirt mustard on their shirts (and even on one occasion at a passerby).

But soon enough, avarice resurfaced and Dr. Nefarious targeted Bill, one of his frequent customers, as one upon whom he would try out a more profitable use of his bratwurst-brain-ray. For weeks leading up to the planned date of attack, Dr. Nefarious made Bill various offers, from napkins, to free desserts, to expensive side-dishes; and he found that whenever Bill was to decline an offer, he would slightly wink his left eye two seconds before declining the offer. This was just a physical tick that Bill had. Whenever he had a negative feeling about an offer being made to him, but before actually declining it or deciding to decline it, he would exhibit this feature, namely, a slightly winked left eye.

So the day of attack came, and Dr. Nefarious reviewed to himself his sinister and diabolical scheme. He would offer Bill a bag of potato chips for twenty dollars and if he saw Bill wink, he would shoot him with his bratwurst-brain-ray and make him buy the chips at the elevated price. On the other hand, if it happened, by chance, that Bill was so utterly famished that he would freely buy the chips for twenty dollars, then Dr. Nefarious would just sell Bill the chips with no brain-ray activity. It's lunch time now and Bill approaches. He buys his normal bratwurst and Dr. Nefarious offers him the outrageously-priced bag of chips. Bill is hungry and he buys them. There are no winks or brain-ray blastings, just a hungry and impetuous Bill. Bill went into this situation with no alternate possibilities. He could not have chosen to refrain from buying the chips. Had he shown any sign of frugality, Dr. Nefarious would have zapped him. And yet, I think all of us would want to say that Bill freely chose the chips. He was not coerced into buying the chips and he had no knowledge of the secret workings of the frankfurter stand. He simply did what he wanted. I call that story my frankfurter-style example[7] of why the thesis of alternate possibilities is limited."

B.F.: "I'll have to think more about this example, but I can tell you right off the bat that the whole idea of Bill having a physical tick, which always precedes his declining of an offer, well . . . it's quite behavioristic. I think I like it."[8]

7. Robert Audi, ed., *The Cambridge Dictionary of Philosophy 2nd edition* (Cambridge University Press, 1999), 323.

". . . Frankfurt-style cases (developed by Harry G. Frankfurt) are situations where an agent acts in accord with his desires and choices, but because of the presence of a counterfactual intervener—a mechanism that would have prevented the agent from doing any alternative action had he shown signs of acting differently—the agent could not have done otherwise. Frankfurt's intuition is that the agent is as responsible as he would have been if there were no intervener, and thus that responsible action does not require alternative possibilities."

8. Behaviorism comprises the thesis that all theories should have observational correlates and that there are no philosophical differences between publicly observable processes (such as actions) and privately observable processes (such as thinking).

Wesley: "I'm not convinced. I think Bill did in fact have alternate possibilities before him. The proverbial 'fork in the road' comes before the offer for chips. Bill could either wink or not wink."

Rachel, nodding this whole time, quite by accident grunts in affirmation to Wes' point. Afterwards, having drawn the attention of the table, she blushes and asks to be excused for a refill of coffee.

Wesley: Capitalizing on the moment, Wesley adds, "As a matter of fact, I think this would be a good time to tell my own story. I would love to get your feedback on it. Would you mind, Calvin?" Calvin grins and tacitly bids Wes to begin.

Wesley: "Ok, let us say that our esteemed physics professor, Dr. Buridan, walks into my philosophy lecture. He enters the room and finds himself (1) fascinated by my lecture, (2) terribly fatigued, and (3) looking for the closest seat to rest himself."

B.F.: "To rest his fat . . ."

Calvin: "Hey! Let's not get personal here."

Wesley: "Actually B.F, that plays perfectly into my story. Thank you. *Buridan's behind* [9], if you will, has a decision to make. It desires to sit and wants to do so by the path of least resistance, namely, choosing the closest seat. However, in this scenario, Buridan's behind finds itself equidistant from each of the two available chairs in the room. So, given what Calvin said earlier about every action having a sufficient cause, towards which of the chairs will Buridan's behind advance? It has no reason to leave the room, as it

9. Buridan's ass (donkey) is a classic illustration of a paradox in philosophy of free will. It refers to a hypothetical situation wherein an ass is placed precisely midway between a two stacks of hay. Since the paradox assumes the ass will always go to whichever pile is closer, it will die standing between these two piles of food since it cannot make any rational decision to choose one over the other.

is fascinated by my lecture . . . insofar as a backside can be fascinated by philosophy. It has no reason to move towards either chair, since each is equidistant from it and offers no special enticement. And, finally, it *has* reason not to continue standing, as it is fatigued. So I ask again, what becomes of Buridan's behind?"

Calvin: "An impertinent question in my mind."

Wesley: "But don't you see, Calvin? My example, in a certain respect, is the exact opposite yours. In the story you shared with us, Bill had a definitive desire for X, but had no alternate possibilities before him. In my story, Buridan's behind has alternate possibilities, but no definitive desire. Buridan's behind is stuck in an equilibrium position and, given your view of reasons as sufficient causes for action, he will never get out."

B.F.: "In my opinion, Buridan would die standing there. And it serves him right for coming in late anyhow." B.F. grins and chuckles a bit to himself.

"Not to change the subject Wes, but I'm not in the habit of deciphering the psychological states of other men's hindquarters. And to boot, I'm having trouble staying focused. A quick break is in order."

B.F. gets up from the table. Calvin and Wes continue just as earnestly in their discussion, unperturbed by the movement and noise around them. By the time B.F. returns, he finds the others in full discussion.

Calvin: "All I'm saying Wes, is that the deep-self arguments one finds in the compatibilist literature[10] can bring some clarity to the issue. But . . . ," Calvin pauses as he notices Rachel return to the table, "I think I should go ahead and wrap things up so we can hear your case tonight, Wes."

10. Harry Frankfurt, "*Freedom of the Will and the Concept of a Person*" in Gary Watson ed., Free Will, (Oxford: University press, 2003), 322–36.

Wesley nods in approbation, though reluctantly. He was enjoying the argument and saw an end in sight. It's a sad reality that these discussions so often stop, in the author's opinion, at the uttermost edges of the puzzle. To be sure, we humans can dive deep into the crushing blackness of the ocean and see wonders shrouded there to which the sun itself has not been privy. But, we must eventually come up for air. We are but mortals, with frailties and limitations just as great as our ambitions for knowledge. It has been wisely said, "For now we see in a mirror dimly. . . ."[11] This statement is a lucid lens into the human condition, and the reader would do well to remember it.

Calvin resumes, "So, I would like to conclude my talk tonight by stressing the utter significance and value of morality for me, both personally and philosophically. As I prepared for tonight's meeting through study and reflection, I found that one of the chief differences between compatibilists and hard determinists was the compatibilists' general commitment to morality. Certainly in my case, I want to affirm that I believe in moral truths and obligations, but I wanted, as well, to show tonight that compatibilism is not violent toward morality. Indeed, I would say that if there were some a-logical motivation for my holding the compatibilist position, if there were some emotional driver lying below the surface of my reason in the recesses of my subconscious that exerts itself upon my will, leading me to this conception of freedom, it would be this, namely, that I cannot allow ethics to be toppled by determinism. I will not place morality's throne outside the city walls. I cannot allow my heart and soul, the thing of which I would say I am the most sure in life, to sit in such a precarious spot."

11. 1 Corinthians 13:11–13.

B.F.: "But you cannot protect it any longer, Calvin. The emperor isn't wearing any clothes and there's no use denying the fact."

Wesley, with his generous frame, shuffled himself about in his chair. He then stroked his heavy beard, blinked his eyes fairly rapidly, and weighed the appropriateness – in his own mind- of interjecting a final point of contention on this most delicate subject. His countenance passed from equivocal to resolute and he began to begin, in which direction we will never know. For it was at this very instant that Rachel interjected her timid, but astute observation.

Rachel: "I was wondering, Professor. If determinism were true, what difference would there be between a moral failing and a physical handicap? What distinction could be drawn between an ugly nose and . . . ."

B.F.: ". . . an ugly character," B.F. interrupts.

Wesley: Filled with pride and overflowing with encouragement, Wesley adds, "Rachel, you are quite clever. Fantastic question! What do you say there Calvin?"

Calvin: "Indeed, she's the brightest of all my students. That's why I invited her to tonight's discussion."

B.F.: "He meant 'what do you say about Rachel's question?'"

Calvin: "Ah, that . . . ."

B.F.: "Let me help. The answer is, for anyone who believes in determinism, that there is no difference. We inherit both bad noses and unseemly characters; and our moral constitution, just as our DNA, is the byproduct of circumstance. So, let's rephrase Rachel's question for Calvin to make it simpler. Would you punish someone for having an ugly nose?"

Calvin: "What a preposterous question! I . . . ." Calvin pauses, and stops himself from responding in the emotions that were, at that moment, coursing through him. He resumes, temperedly, "I would not punish someone for a bad nose nor for hiding their nose with a bad moustache." Calvin grins, feeling he had regained some honor from the indirect insult on B.F.

B.F. sat up straight in his chair and his moustache, and by that I mean B.F. himself, seemed to flare and quiver with ferocious ire.

Wesley: Summoning his genial baritone, Wesley mediates, "Well, then. I am very anxious to move on to my portion of the evening. If you'll do me the pleasure, I'd like to dive right into my arguments. Otherwise, I fear we'll have to continue this at my home, and my cat does not like visitors," he jokes.

Calvin: "Yes, please let's keep things moving along. I'm going to get myself a coffee refill and we'll begin straightaway."

Further Reading: Compatibilism

Gary Watson: *Agency and Answerability* (Oxford: Clarendon Press, 2004)

John Martin Fischer: *The Metaphysics of Free Will* (Oxford: Blackwell Publishers, 1994)

Daniel Dennett: *Elbow Room* (Cambridge: MIT Press, 1984)

Dialogue 3

Would the Real Morally Responsible Agent Please Stand Up?

All things therefore seemed to point to this; that I was slowly losing hold of my original and better self, and becoming slowly incorporated with my second and worse. Between these two, I now felt I had to choose.

—ROBERT LOUIS STEVENSON, *THE STRANGE CASE OF DR. JEKYLL AND MR. HYDE*

Two roads diverged in a yellow wood, And sorry I could not travel both . . .

—ROBERT FROST, *THE ROAD NOT TAKEN*

WESLEY WAS STOUT IN both character and frame. He had a full, thick beard, a bump of a nose, and two large affable eyes, whose gaze warmed all who passed before it. He was jovial and passionate. And though he bore all the hallmarks of a discombobulated bachelor - mismatched socks, which disclosed themselves quite early in the evening by cause of

Wes' short-legged pants, and a handful of seemingly random notes scratched on the back or side of various paper media- his preparedness and genius could not be mistaken, or underestimated. Wesley also had the pleasant quirk, as his students would say, of seamlessly transitioning his verbiage from pedantic to colloquial in a single phrase.

When Calvin returned to the table, he sat down to another string of B.F.'s philosophy jokes.

B.F.: "So, what did the Buddhist say to the hotdog vendor? – Make me one with everything?" Again B.F. laughed all over himself. Rachel laughs as well, although not at the joke. She finds the manner in which B.F.'s nose seems to perch upon his fluttering moustache simply hilarious. They all enjoy a good laugh. All except Calvin, that is. His eyes and attention reverted back to that triple-sided tabletop menu and most importantly to the words decoratively inscribed thereupon: *La Fontaine Inattendue.*

There was something enigmatic about this French phrase that would not loosen its grip on his regard or attention. He mumbled to himself a possible clue, "The unexpected source . . . ,"but his train of thought was derailed by Wesley.

Wesley: "Calvin, B.F., Rachel, are you all ready to begin? Well, first things first, it's best we start with confession." Wesley grins at Rachel, as if to invite her into his playfulness. "I confess: we Libertarians are control freaks. Libertarians are, in point of fact, all about control. The truth or falsity of determinism is a point of contention for us only because we see it diminishing a person's control over her actions. Control is the heartbeat of our movement. Control, as I hope to show later on, is what will give us morality, responsibility, and true freedom. But before I get ahead of myself, let me give you a general agenda for my talk tonight. I would like to

1. give you an outline of the various libertarian accounts of free will,

2. explain which account I hold to and my reasons for it, and

3. delineate the numerous reasons why I think libertarian freedom is the most rational choice available to us.

Alright then, so to begin I would like to outline the three main types of Libertarianism that I find present in the literature. They all seek to answer one fundamental question: How can we explain the causation of actions, without recourse to determinism, and in a way that will allow the agent to have real control over her thoughts, beliefs, and behavior?

The first of the three Libertarian conceptions of freedom is what I would call an event-causal view. This school of thought holds that our actions are caused, as the name implies, by events. This may sound familiar. And it should, because this is the exact same claim that determinists make: our actions are caused by prior events, whether prior desires, reasons, or physical events. This makes sense, since we do see a correlation between events and the actions of people in the real world. People are more likely to make certain decisions if they have certain events in their backgrounds. For example, I am more likely to prefer wine to Coca-Cola, as a beverage at dinner, if I am born in France as compared to America. Or, likewise, one is more likely to be sexually deviant in one's adulthood if one was molested as a child. So it's clear that prior events have a bearing on our decisions. However, there is one large difference between event-causal libertarianism and determinism, and that is for the event-causal libertarian, the events that cause our actions only cause them nondeterministically."

Calvin "Now, hold on just a minute, Wesley! What does it mean for a cause to be nondeterministic? Isn't that tantamount to saying it's no cause at all? In my thesaurus, 'to cause' and 'to determine' are synonyms. So when you say to me, 'these causes are nondeterministic', I hear 'these causes are non-causes.' Aren't you contradicting yourself, lad?"

Wesley: "Far from it! Nondeterministic causes are widely accepted phenomena. A nondeterministic cause is a cause that is necessary, but not sufficient."

B.F.: "Maybe the indeterminate cause alone is not sufficient, but the conglomeration of necessary and indeterminate causes form a sufficient and deterministic causal group, such that the parts are all insufficient individually to bring about the outcome, but as a group they are sufficient and the outcome is, thus, determined."

Calvin: "I hate to admit it, but I think B.F. has a good point here. How could we explain an event if all its preceding causes were not sufficient for the occurrence of that event? Where did it come from? Why did it happen?"[1]

Wesley: "If you obfuscate the difference between 'to cause' and 'to determine', you get your stuff messed up. As it is, I don't like this version of libertarianism anyhow, so I'll concede your point for time's sake.

Moving on - the second conception of libertarianism I'd like to cover is called the agent-causal view. This position

1. "It might be accepted that nondeterministically caused events can be explained but objected that they cannot be completely or fully or adequately explained because it cannot be explained why they had to happen. But the question why such an event had to happen carries a false presupposition; the event did not have to happen. And it is no incompleteness or inadequacy in an explanation that it fails to answer to a false presupposition . . ."

Randolph Clarke, *Libertarian Accounts of Free Will* (Oxford: Oxford University Press, 2003), p.36.

is radically different from determinism, for it postulates a new kind of cause: the agent." Wesley looks at Rachel again and, with a sly and sarcastic grin, jokes, "Now these aren't FBI agents we're talking about here, but rather persons and such in the most robust sense. These persons are substances, different from and not reducible to their brains. They have abilities. And one of these abilities is to cause or to decide, totally outside of the influence of prior events. They are unhampered, uninfluenced, Socratic-ponderers, always in a state of neutrality and rationality."

B.F.: "Hogwash!" B.F. quickly picks up his empty coffee mug and looks inside. It was unclear whether his comment was addressed to Wesley or the coffee mug.

Calvin: "I have two quick questions for you, Wes. When you say 'substance', are you referring to it in the same way as the substance-dualism advocates whom I'm teaching about in class? If so, how do you get around the difficulties they face?"

Wesley notices Rachel's puzzled look.

Wesley: "Good question! Let me first outline that difficulty for Rachel and then I will answer your question as best as I can, Calvin. Ok, so substance-dualists believe that persons are composed of two essential parts: body and spirit. Uh . . . more specifically, substance-dualists believe that one's brain is a material substance and one's mind is a mental substance and that these two substances interact and are distinct. The problem comes when they attempt to sketch *how* the two substances interact. How does a spirit or mind, which has no material parts, cause something to happen in the body, which is a material thing? I don't presume to be able to answer every metaphysical question this evening, but I will say that for a Christian theist like myself, the substance-dualism discussion poses less of a problem."

Rachel: "Why is that, professor?"

Wesley: "Well Rachel, as a Christian theist I already believe that God, who by his very nature is an immaterial substance, is causally active in our material world. Given the manifold reasons I have for this belief, I see no issue in admitting that I don't understand the logistics of how non-material substances interact with material ones. But who cares?! You'd have to be a real nincompoop to jettison a belief you're certain of for another one with smoother edges."

B.F.: "For those who hold to an agent-causal view, how do they make sense of the clear connection, which you admitted to earlier, between prior events and the actions of the agent? It seems that agent-causal libertarians are on the horns of a dilemma. Either, (1) they must say that prior events cause the agent-substance to cause the action, or (2) prior events have no bearing on the agent's causing of the action. If (1) is true, then we have determinism, albeit with one extra step thrown into the mix. In the place of 'prior events causing a brain state in the person, which causes an action by the person', we have 'prior events causing the agent to cause a brain state in the person, which causes the action by the person.' On the other hand, if (2) is true, there's a total disconnect between events and reasons and an agent's choice. Therefore a person's choosing is utterly arbitrary, not based upon or influenced by their upbringing, culture, or education. This, as I think you would have to admit Wesley, is empirically untenable."

Calvin: "It's true Wes. The agent-causal view is on the horns of a nasty dilemma."

Wesley: "I agree."

Calvin and B.F. exchange a baffled gaze.

Wesley: "That's why I hold to a hybrid view,[2] which is the third view I wished to talk about this evening. The

2. For a summary of the hybrid view, see Randolph Clarke, *Libertarian Accounts of Free Will* (Oxford: Oxford University Press, 2003),

hybrid view takes the best of the event-causal and agent-causal views and, in my humble opinion, sidesteps the problems that creep up in both. The event-causal view has the strength that one's reasons are causally connected with one's actions, which is what we all see in others and experience in ourselves. However, it has the downside of not giving us control of our actions. Since events are the only causes factoring into which actions we perform, agents do not control their actions in the strong sense that we would like to show. On the contrary, the agent-causal view has the advantage of giving the agent full control of his or her actions, with the downside of offering no explanation of how reasons or events can influence decisions. The hybrid view states, quite simply, that there are two types of causes which are both necessary, but not sufficient in themselves for free action to occur, namely, events and the agent herself. Therefore, events or reasons are necessary but not sufficient for free action. Agent causal force is necessary, but not sufficient for free action. Together, they provide the necessary and sufficient condition for free action to occur. This just makes common sense to me. Someone has reasons and influences acting upon him and in him, but those reasons will not actualize into action apart from a movement of that person's will."

Calvin, intrigued by Wes' elucidation of the thesis, encouraged him to proceed to his closing arguments for the truthfulness of libertarian freedom. B.F. checked his watch.

Wesley: "Righto. To begin my closing remarks, I would like to quote one of my favorite authors, Mortimer J. Adler,

"The real existence of instances of [metaphysical entities] can be posited only on the grounds that, if they did

---

pp. 151–52.

not exist, the observed phenomena could not be adequately explained."[3]

Free will is a metaphysical concept. I believe it because it is the only possible foundation for the other beliefs that I hold to be true. If there were no libertarian freedom, I could see no way on maintaining the robust brand of morality that I find intuitive. If there were no libertarian freedom, I could not make sense of deliberation.[4] Moreover, as a Christian, I cannot get around the fact that libertarian freedom plays a crucial role in theodicy, which is our answer to the problem of evil.[5] Libertarian freedom is the only kind of free will that will allow for the retributive justice we see in the scriptures. I wouldn't punish my daughter for having a big nose and, similarly, I don't suppose God would pour his wrath out on some poor, wretched creature for all eternity for something that was outside her control. Moreover, in daily interaction in society, free will is a necessary component. It is the basis 'for the desert of praise and blame, reward and punishment, and for the full appropriateness of certain reactive attitudes – such as pride and remorse, gratitude and resentment, moral approbation and disapprobation . . .'"[6]

3. Mortimer Adler, *Ten Philosophical Mistakes*, (New York: Touchstone,1985), p.49.

4. ". . . determinism is self-stultifying. If my mental processes are totally determined, I am totally determined either to accept or to reject determinism. But if the sole reason for my believing or not believing X is that I am causally determined to believe it I have no ground for holding that my judgment is true or false."

H.P. Owen, *Christian Theism*, (Edinburgh: T & T Clark, 1984), p.118.

5. For more on this see Alvin Plantinga, *God, Freedom, and Evil*, (Grand Rapids: Eerdmans Publishing, 1974).

6. Randolph Clarke, *Libertarian Accounts of Free Will* (Oxford: Oxford University Press, 2003), p.6.

Wesley observes Rachel scratching down some of his points. He recapitulates for her benefit.

"You could think of my argument as an example of the classical argument form *Modus Tollens*.[7] My argument could go thusly:

If Determinism, then moral nihilism.

Not moral nihilism.

Therefore, not determinism.[8]

All of that to say that if I were to accept determinism, I would at the same time have to accept that I am largely, if not entirely, deluded about the majority of my most foundational beliefs. So, clearly, it would take a preponderance of evidence to counteract the case against determinism. What is the proof of determinism? I don't know of any."

B.F.: "I think the inability of philosophers to come up with a cogent version of libertarianism counts for the truthfulness of determinism. Normally, I admit, disproving hypothesis X would not offer support to hypothesis Y. However, given that a man is either free or not free – there is no middle case – a lowering probability for the truthfulness of one, necessarily, increases the probability of the other. For example, if a man's chances of dying double, his chances of living are halved. This should be admitted."

Calvin: "Wes, I don't believe this hybrid version gets you totally off the horns of the dilemma. So you've shown how reasons can factor into the equation for the agent. That's great. But if an agent decides to act because of the reasons she has, would you not say that those very reasons

---

7. If P then Q, Not Q, Therefore not P. It is also referred to as "denying the consequent."

8. This syllogism is a short way of saying that, "If determinism were true then moral nihilism would also be true. I know that moral nihilism is not true. Therefore, determinism is not true either."

determined her action? Were they not, all together, the efficient cause[9] for her acting?"

Wesley: "I'm glad you brought this up Calvin, because this is a common misunderstanding. And since we're speaking Aristotelian, I'll answer you in like kind. Reasons function not as efficient causes, but as final causes.[10] And yes, when a person acts, they act *because* of their reasons. But don't let the language deceive you to believe that the word 'because' here denotes determinism! Trying to show that determinism is a truth of language will get us nowhere. No, we must go deeper than linguistic subterfuge to found our understanding of human action. To be sure, people act for various reasons: self-aggrandizement, jealousy, hate, love, the common good. Men ask themselves what kind of men they want to be. They ask themselves what kind of men they in fact are."

Rachel: "You know, professor, my boyfriend was just telling me about some studies done on the topic of psychological anchoring. He said that psychologists have done thorough statistical studies and found that when people make decisions that they themselves believe to be only one-off decisions, they are in fact building their own characters and shaping their own self-perceptions. The studies showed that a person who steals in a particular instance will be more likely the next time to perform the same action. Vice versa, the person who refrains from stealing in a particular instance will be less likely to steal when a second

9. "An efficient cause is that by means of which an effect is produced."

J. P. Moreland & William Lane Craig, *Philosophical Foundations for a Christian Worldview*, (Downers Grove: Intervarsity Press, 2003), 276.

10. ". . . a final cause is that for the sake of which an effect is produced." Ibid., 276.

opportunity comes around. I guess it has something to do with the kind of person they believe themselves to be."

Wesley: "Interesting comment, Rachel. That is so very relevant to our topic. People act for the reasons they have and their actions become reasons they will access for future action. Or, said differently, I may have reasons A, B, and C to do an action X. But once I do X, X will now enter the repertoire of my reasons for any future similar actions, and so forth. So I build my character as I go and form the person I am by the choices I make. It all becomes, as you said, intimately tied to our self-identities . . . . You know, this all reminds me of a certain act in one of my favorite musicals: *Les Miserables.* M. Madeleine, the main character of the novel-made-musical, was an escaped convict, formerly named Jean Valjean, who turned his life over to God and changed for the good. However, several years later – decades even – he was faced with a moral crossroads. He, now a respectable man and the mayor of a small town, was in court watching another man be tried and convicted for his own (Madeleine's) past crimes. At this point in the musical, he wrestles with who he is, and what he is to do in this situation . . . . I haven't forgotten the words to his song. Let me repeat them for you.

> 'He thinks that man is me! He knew him at a glance! That stranger he has found. This man could be my chance.
>
> Why should I save his hide? Why should I right this wrong? When I have come so far and struggled for so long? If I speak, I am condemned! If I stay silent, I am damned!
>
> I am the master of hundreds of workers. They all look to me. How can I abandon them, how can they live, if I am not free? If I speak, I am condemned! If I stay silent, I am damned!
>
> *Who am I?*

Can I condemn this man to slavery, pretend I
do not see his agony? This innocent who bears
my face, who goes to judgment in my place.
Who am I?
Can I conceal myself forevermore? Pretend
I'm not the man I was before? And must my
name until I die be no more than an alibi? Must
I lie?
How can I ever face my fellow man? How can
I ever face myself again?
My soul belongs to God, I know. I made that
bargain long ago. He gave me hope, when hope
was gone. He gave me strength to journey on.
Who am I? Who am I?
I am Jean Valjean!'[11]

. . . So, you see, we all have these moments,
moments of moral crossroads, moments where we
make ourselves."[12]

Calvin: "But doesn't the original set of reasons necessitate this cascade of action, anchoring, and more action?"

Wesley: "That's the million dollar question, Calvin.
I don't think they do for the reasons I've outlined. It's my
opinion that an agent, at any given moment, has reasons
pressing in on him to act in mutually exclusive ways. What
tips the scale to create action? Is it a positive surplus in one
category of reasons versus another, say 'to sit right now' versus 'to stand up right now'? Or, is it that a deliberative agent

---

11. http://en.wikiquote.org/wiki/Les_Mis%C3%A9rables_(musical)

12. "This condition of Ultimate Responsibility, or UR, does not
require that we could have done otherwise (AP) for every act done
of our own free wills. But it does require that we could have done
otherwise with respect to some acts in our past life histories by which
we formed our present characters. I call these earlier acts by which we
formed our present characters 'self-forming actions,' or SFA's."

Robert Kane, John Martin Fischer, Derk Pereboom, Manuel
Vargas, *Four Views on Free Will*, (Blackwell, 2007), 14.

exercises his causal influence and chooses which reasons he will prefer and act upon? Philosophy has escorted us far, but I suggest that now we look further into our Christian theology and even into the Scriptures to see whether we can find some more conclusive direction."

B.F.: "My *'leave right now'* category of reasons just went positive."

Calvin: "You know you are always welcome to stay, B.F."

Wesley: "Yes, we may have different opinions about God, but that doesn't mean we're forcing you out when we want to talk about him."

B.F.: "Actually, I have a prior engagement, fellows. And as always, I appreciate being released from the religious dialogue for which I have no interest whatsoever."

Calvin: "Well, if you change your mind, the door is always open."

Before the other three could bat an eye, B.F. had lassoed himself with his scarf, resettled in his coat, and was out the door. Wesley looked to Rachel and Calvin, excited about what was in store.

Coffeehouse Compatibilism

Further Reading: Libertarianism

Robert Kane: *The Oxford Handbook of Free Will*, (ed.) (Oxford: Oxford University Press, 2002)

Robert Kane: *The Significance of Free Will* (Oxford: Oxford University Press, 1996)

Timothy O'Connor: *Persons and Causes* (Oxford: Oxford University Press, 2000)

Randolph Clarke: *Libertarian Accounts of Free Will* (Oxford: Oxford University Press, 2003)

Peter Van Inwagen: *An Essay on Free Will* (Oxford: Clarendon Press, 2002)

Dialogue 4

Compatibilism and the Christian Story

The truth of the matter, however, is that Scripture does not say what sort of freedom we have; it only teaches that we are free . . . we must argue the case for a particular kind of free will inferentially from other truths taught by Scripture which best fit our notion of freedom.

—JOHN S. FEINBERG, *NO ONE LIKE HIM*

Does it follow from: 'Turn Ye' that therefore you can turn? Does it follow from: 'Love the Lord thy God with all thy heart' that therefore you can love with all your heart?

—MARTIN LUTHER, *BONDAGE OF THE WILL*

RAISING THE SQUARE COFFEEHOUSE napkin to her youthful lips, Rachel delicately dabbed away the drizzle of beverage. And in that moment, Calvin, in happy coincidence, caught a glimpse of that familiar and enigmatic French phrase upon the napkin, which Rachel unknowingly advertised. Time abated in its expeditious course and Calvin stared at the gaudy font for days, or so it seemed.

La Fontaine Inattendue

The elusive message lay before him, tempting him as an unopened letter bearing his name. And yet, he was unable to discern its riddle. He knew only that its disclosure would be shocking and good.

Wesley: "As Christians, I think it's only proper that we invite the Lord's direction as we pursue these questions further. Calvin, would you be willing to pray to God on our behalf?"

Calvin: "Certainly," Calvin responds, pulling himself from his thoughtful ponderings. He folds his hands and reverently bows his head. "Dear Lord, you are the king of all wisdom and knowledge. There is no subject, no field of study that falls outside the scope of your comprehensive genius. We would be ridiculously remiss if we neglected to tap into your providential guidance this evening. And so we beseech you Father, before we continue in our discussion, for your direction and insight. Help us to hear wisdom's call, from whichever direction or source she summons. We ask this for your honor and our benefit, in Jesus' name. Amen."

Rachel looked proudly upon Calvin, appreciating the fact that he, as a scholar, both loved God and was not ashamed to show it.

Wesley: "Thank you, Calvin. Before we jump headfirst into what I'm sure is going to be an excellent and exhilarating exchange, I would like to get your opinion on something. What do you think *the Scriptures* say about this issue of freedom?"

Calvin: "My reading of Scripture paints a picture of a God who controls all things. He is sovereign over all peoples, worlds, and governments. He ordains all events; and his providential control extends even to the minutiae of life, such as the roll of a die[1] or the flight path of a stray arrow.[2] There is nothing that falls outside the purview of his divine decree. I think that, in deciding upon the issue of freedom, we must reckon with the God of the Bible. And he is a God who controls the world and who knows all future events."

Wesley: "And do you think that God's control and knowledge entail determinism?"

Calvin: "I wouldn't say they entail it, no. But they certainly make it more likely."

Wesley: "Obviously, I also believe in the truths you just mentioned. But I ask that question because I know of at least one philosophical framework for making sense of God's knowledge of the future and his sovereign control of everything, which do not entail determinism; it's called middle knowledge.[3] So, at a minimum, we Christians are not constrained to a deterministic philosophy, even if we believe God knows and controls absolutely *all* things."

Calvin: "We may not be logically constrained, but you know as well as I do, Wesley, that these frameworks are debatable. One could say that Libertarians are only augmenting layers to their free will theory in the same way a developing child makes supplementary theories for why Santa did not eat his cookies this year or how Santa can enter houses without chimneys. You have one dubious theory which you tack onto another, always answering the objections left by the first theory and creating new objections and questions for the second."

Wesley: "I hardly think explaining the philosophical underpinning of our ideas should be equated with this manner of juvenile hedging."

1. Luke 1:19.

2. 1 Kings 22:34.

3. See William Lane Craig, *The Only Wise God*, (Eugene: Wipf and Stock, 2000), pgs. 119–52.

Calvin: "I guess it depends on one's vantage point . . ."

Wesley: "Since we're talking about hedging, Calvin, what would convince you of Libertarian free will?! You must admit to some possible argument that would cause a change of heart on your side. I'm assuming my arguments thus far this evening have fallen short of this goal. So, what would be sufficient evidence? Or are you, yourself, simply *hedging* your own position?"

Calvin: "By God's grace, I hope never to be so unyieldingly dogmatic! I suppose I would recant of my compatibilism if you were to show me an unambiguous, explicit, biblical passage that either clearly taught libertarian free will or logically implied it with such lucidity that it could not be denied."

Wesley: "A tall order, indeed!"

Calvin: "Perhaps, and yet possible."

Wesley: "I'd say it's unlikely to find such a passage. It's hard to imagine a verse that would not contain some smidgen of ambiguity, such that interpretation would be unequivocal."

Calvin heard a rustling coming from across the table. He turned towards it in curiosity. It was Rachel. Wesley and Calvin both stopped talking and looked at her to see what was the matter with their, heretofore, quiet and cool-headed companion. Apparently, in a flash of movement, she had toppled her espresso and spilt a good amount of it onto the table. There was not so much liquid that it risked running over onto anyone, nor was there really enough to cause any substantial mess, but it was just enough – in the author's opinion – to drown an idea. And that's just what it did.

Rummaging for some extra napkins in her purse, she frantically disposed its contents upon the table. Lipstick, cellphone, compact mirror, make-up paraphernalia, gum, car keys, a hair brush, and some coinage all tossed successively onto the table. Finally, she retrieved the napkins. But pausing, she placed them aside and removed a book from the bottom of her purse, pulled out the bookmark and looked upon it. It bore a frilly ribbon, an inscription, and a picture of two open hands in the backdrop. She stared for some time. She thought. She tilted her head and looked at Calvin. Soberly and humbly, she returned Calvin's inquisitive gaze.

Rachel: "I think I know of such a biblical passage, professor," Rachel offered.

Calvin leaned back in his chair, bracing himself for what was to come.

Wesley: Wesley coached her on. "Please share, Rachel. Please share."

Rachel: "First Corinthians 10:13:

> No temptation has overtaken you that is not common to man. God is faithful, and he will not let you be tempted beyond your ability, *but with the temptation he will also provide the way of escape*, that you may be able to endure it.

This bookmark was a gift from a friend. It's a reminder to me that no matter what temptations I face, God will always provide me a way of escaping sin. It's a token that my freedom in Christ is a *freedom from sinning*."

Calvin: "I'm not sure I follow."

Rachel: "Well, I may be wrong professors, but from my understanding of tonight's discussion, a verse would show that Christians are free if it were to show two real possible paths of action. I believe this verse shows just that very thing."

Wesley: "Goodness gracious, the girl's right! If a Christian person is free from sin,[4] which they are - God be praised - they cannot be determined beforehand to commit sin."

---

4. This is the explicit teaching of Romans Chapters 6 & 7.

Calvin: "Now slow down a second! Explain to me how this defeats compatibilism."

Wesley: "Let me say it in a different way, Calvin. Let's imagine that you were faced with a moral choice yesterday at noon. You could either steal B.F.'s nose hair trimmer or not. Let us also imagine that you are a Christian in this scenario. We have a direct biblical promise that God will not allow you to be tempted beyond your ability to refrain from sinning. So we know that you have a real possibility and promise of acting otherwise than sinning. If you do sin, and steal the nose hair trimmer, when you look back upon this occurrence, you can know that you did not *have* to sin. You could have done otherwise. You could have refrained. You could have walked the path of obedience."

Wesley stops, pulls out his pen, and draws a small forking path on his paper. On one fork he writes, "Path to Sin." One the other side, he writes, "Path of escape."

Wes resumes, "According to our scenario, at noon yesterday you reached a fork in the road. There were two possibilities before you. You had all the grace and freedom to choose the path of escape, which is the path of obedience. It's God's promise that you are not causally determined to sin. Think of it this way. If you were causally determined to sin at noon yesterday, how could the verse be true, as it says '. . . he will not allow you to be tempted beyond your ability'?"

Calvin: "And what if this verse means something else entirely? We shouldn't base such a substantial belief on just one verse." [5]

---

5. The following rebuttal could be given for my proposed reading of 1 Corinthians 10:13 and the argument for Libertarian freedom that follows from said reading: 1 Corinthians 10:1–14 is speaking specifically about idolatry. Since this is the case, the contender may say, 1 Corinthians 10:13 is not dealing with the temptation to sin *generally*, but only the specific temptation to sin in apostasy (i.e. giving up the faith). So, 1 Corinthians 10:13 means that God will give *the Elect* the

Wesley: "Indeed, we should not. However, listen to me, my friend. Is this verse not simply a summary of what other passages in Romans and elsewhere in the New Testament teach us? Doesn't this verse communicate what we both believe theologically, namely, the *freedom from sin for believers*? Assuredly, you do not deny this fundament point of doctrine. . . . if I'm not mistaken, it's even taught in the Westminster confession!"[6]

---

grace to persevere unto the end (i.e. Perseverance of the Saints) and never let them be effactually tempted to give up their faith. It does not touch on, however, the issue of whether Christians can refrain from everyday sins.

There are two things I would like to say about this possible rebuttal:

(1) Because the 'freedom in Christ from sin' motif is taught elsewhere in Scripture (most notably in Romans 6 & 7), I find this rejoinder mostly irrelevant.

"What has [justification] to do with life in this present age? Anything? Everything, Paul asserts in Rom. 6. Christ's death 'on our behalf' frees us not only from the penalty of sin but from the power of sin also . . . . Subduing the power of sin is the topic in Rom. 6." Douglas Moo, *The First Epistle to the Romans*, The New International Commentary of the New Testament, (Eerdmans Publishing, 1996), 350.

(2) Biblical scholarship on this passage (1 Corinthians 10:13) is not favorable to the reading put forward in the rebuttal.

"The 'trial' or 'temptation' probably harks back to the sins enumerated in vv. 7–10 . . . . Paul's point, then, is that in *ordinary human trials* one can expect divine aid." Gordon Fee, *The First Epistle to the Corinthians*, The New International Commentary of the New Testament, (Eerdmans Publishing, 1987), 460–61.

6. Douglas Moo, in his commentary on Romans, quotes the Westminster Larger Catechism, " Although sanctification be inseparably joined with justification, yet they differ, in that God in justification imputeth the righteousness of Christ; in sanctification his Spirit infuseth grace, and enableth to the exercise thereof; in the former, sin is pardoned; in the other, sin is subdued."

Douglas Moo, *The First Epistle to the Romans*, The New International Commentary of the New Testament, (Eerdmans Publishing, 1996), 350.

Calvin smiled from ear to ear, which he often did when he was shocked at something. This clarion note of truth resounded within his soul and its deafening pitch could not be avoided: *Christians are free.* He tried, however, to regain his composure and offer rebuttal.

Calvin: "And yet this verse, and the argument that admittedly follows from it, only applies to Christians. . . . We shouldn't, we can't, and we shan't make hasty generalizations about all people in all places from such a passage. And unless you propose that free will catches like the flu, I see no reason to accept that Libertarian freedom applies outside the household of faith."

Rachel: "So, Christians are free, but unbelievers are causally determined?"

Wesley: "There's something curious about that idea . . . something almost literary. Two people talking over lunch, one determining her own actions and words and the second being carried along by a wave of preceding influences. One is a captain and the other just a ship."

Calvin: "Yet . . ." Calvin interjects, "as I sit here thinking further about the implications of all Christians being free, I can't help but think that this truth may actually *entail* that non-believers are also free."

Wesley: "How so, Calvin?"

Calvin: "Follow me. If Christian people are truly and *Libertarianly* free, at least during some points in their lives, then they are, by definition, not causally determined to do any certain action at those points."

Wesley: "By definition," Wes echoes.

Calvin: "Yes, and if there are undetermined events in the system at moment T-1, how can we say that at moment T, all was causally determined by events at T-1?"

Rachel: "Run that by me one more time. . . "

Wesley: "I think I understand your point. Since we've introduced non-causally determined events into the system, namely, the actions of Christians, the system can no longer be wholly causally determined. For any event (E) to be causally determined, all events in E's past must also be causally determined.[7] For if there is some event in the causal chain leading to E's generation that might not have happened, then E itself might not have happened. And if one can say of some event that 'it might not have happened', or any number of synonymous locutions: 'it could have been otherwise' or 'it was a real possibility that this event did not obtain', then that event is not causally determined."

Rachel: "Can you give me an example?"

Wesley: "Certainly! We'll do our case study with Oliver the adolescent. Oliver is a believer and, thus, is free. One day, Oliver is presented with a moral choice. He is visiting his nonbelieving girlfriend, Jezebel, at her home while her parents are out. At one distinct moment in the evening (8:01 pm), Oliver is tempted to have sexual relations with Jezebel. We know that at 8:01 pm Oliver has all the grace he needs not to give in to this temptation. So, there are two possible futures, one in which Oliver gives in to the temptation and sleeps with his girlfriend, and another in which he does not. We will allow 'S' to symbolize the act of Oliver sleeping with his girlfriend at 8:01 pm. At any time prior to 8:01 pm, S

7. It could be argued that a group of contingent events might function together as a necessitating or sufficient cause for E. These events would, although themselves contingent and not predetermined, necessarily cause E. The author allows for this possibility. However, my point in the statement above: "For any event (E) to be causally determined, all events in E's past must also be causally determined", was to show the implications of combining the theory of classic determinism with the notion that Christians are Libertarianly free. The laws of nature and the state of the world one year ago could not necessitate E with Libertarianly free creatures in E's causal past. Therefore, E was not predetermined in the classic sense.

is not causally determined to happen, due to Oliver's free will. Since S is not causally determined, Jezebel's part in S is not determined. So, at least some of nonbelieving Jezebel's future actions are contingent."

Rachel: "Okay, so, the bottom line is that the fact that Christians are free means that nonbelievers cannot be causally determined to act."

Calvin: "Yes . . . ."

Rachel: "Wow."

Calvin: "However," Calvin retorts, "this argument only proves that non-believers are not causally determined, and that does not necessarily mean that they are free in the Libertarian sense.[8] What about the other Scriptures that say nonbelievers are slaves of sin and unable to do right in God's sight? What about Augustine's classic treatment of this issue?" Calvin reached into his briefcase, which sat neatly beside his chair. He lay before them the following laminated table.

Pre-Fall Man	Post-Fall Man	Reborn Man	Glorified Man
able to sin	able to sin	able to sin	able to not sin
able to not sin	unable to not sin	able to not sin	unable to sin
posse peccare posse non peccare	non posse non peccare	posse non peccare	non posse peccare

Wesley: "I thought this might come up tonight. This is why . . . ." Wesley, fighting fire with fire, reached into the

8. Being free, in the Libertarian sense, is not the same as not being causally determined. The reader must keep this in mind. One's actions could be random.

front right pocket of his jeans and pulled out an old receipt, on the back of which was written a couple notes, someone's phone number, and the following table.

	Christians	Nonbelievers
1	Not causally determined	Not causally determined
2	Libertarianly free	Libertarianly free
3	Spiritually free	*Not* Spiritually free

Wesley: "There!"

There was a brief moment of silence as each looked over the tables and pondered their meanings.

Wesley: "Calvin, I believe Augustine was right on the money with the delineation shown in this table of yours. He is right when he says that fallen man is unable to choose the good. However, let me explain our disagreement."

Wesley looks over to Rachel. "Rachel, do you remember what the word 'equivocation' meant from your logic course?"

Rachel: "Sure, it's when one uses a term in more than one way in a single context. One funny example I remember from class was a man who said to the police officer, "The sign said 'fine for parking here', and since it was fine, I went ahead and parked.""

Wesley: "This is our problem, Calvin: equivocation. I agree that nonbelievers are unable to refrain from sinning. And I also believe that Christians are free in ways that nonbelievers are not. 'How is that?' you may ask. Let's start from the beginning, as this word 'free' can be a sticky thing. I have argued that both believers and nonbelievers are not causally determined to act in any certain way. In addition to this, I have argued that both are also Libertarianly free, meaning that they control their actions and have real alternate possibilities before them. However, I believe that Christians are spiritually free whereas nonbelievers are not."

Rachel: "What do you mean by spiritually free, professor?"

Wesley: "I was just about to elaborate on that. One is spiritually free when one has God's spirit living inside him/her, fostering holy desires and giving strength to pursue those desires."[9]

So you see, (1) not being causally determined, (2) being Libertarianly free, and (3) being spiritually free are all distinct, albeit interconnected, issues."

Rachel: "In what way are they interconnected?"

Wesley: "Well, at a minimum, each one of the three needs the prior as a necessary condition for its truthfulness. So, for example, the falsity of Determinism is a necessary condition for the truth of Libertarian freedom. And the truth of Libertarian freedom is a necessary condition for the truth of spiritual freedom. One cannot be Libertarianly free if Determinism is true and one cannot be spiritually free if one is not already Libertarianly free.[10] This interconnectedness is one reason why the three definitions have so often been mixed up. Now follow me, holding the position that a nonbeliever is Libertarianly free does not make me Pelagian in my theology, nor does it mean that I am avoiding the clear teaching of the Scriptures on the sinner's

9. I draw this understanding, namely, that being spiritually free is having new God-initiated desires and the strength to act on them, from Romans 6:20, 22; 8:5–8. Additionally, from Philippians 2:13 (NLT), "For God is at work in you, giving you the desire and the power to do what pleases him."

10. This is clear from the fact that a Christian person cannot refrain from sinning at time X, if at X the Christian is either (1) causally determined to sin at X, or (2) simply unable to control their actions at X or any other time (read: "not Libertarianly free").

deadness in sin. The bottom line is that scriptural passages[11] that teach the moral inability of man to meet God's law are not talking about Libertarian freedom. They are dealing with spiritual freedom and Christian Compatibilists have historically equivocated the two meanings. They are not the same thing!"

Wesley, anticipating Rachel's clarifying questions, adds, "By the way, Pelagianism is the belief that original sin did not taint human nature and that our moral will is still capable of choosing the good without special divine aid. I do not believe this! As I said before, I believe nonbelievers are Libertarianly free and, yet, spiritually enslaved and unable to do anything good in God's sight without His direct aid."

Rachel: "But how can someone be free and enslaved all at once?"

Wesley: "Because it is two senses . . . . Picture this Rachel, a nonbeliever (Thomas) walks into an exercise facility. Thomas is Libertarianly free and has many real options before him. He is not causally determined to run on the treadmill or jump rope. He is free. However, Thomas is not physically able to lift the 150 pound dumbbell above his head. So, Thomas is not causally determined, he's Libertarianly free, and yet there is something that he cannot do. In a similar way, when Thomas reaches a moral decision-point in his life without the Holy Spirit living inside of him, he will not be able to do what is good in God's sight. The reason he is not able is that he is not spiritually free; he does not have the Holy Spirit living in him to give him holy desires and the power to act on them."[12]

11. 1 Corinthians 2:14, John 8:34–48, Romans 3:10–11, Romans 8: 7–8, Ephesians 2:1–3.

12. See also Titus 1:15 & Romans 14:23. In addition to the example above, I believe this has a lot to do with God's categorical assignment as sinful of all the actions of nonbelievers given their

Calvin: "How about a real life example where Thomas reaches a moral crossroads as a nonbeliever?"

Wesley: "In a way, Calvin, your question is misleading. If Thomas is a nonbeliever, then the Scripture says that he is a slave to sin, cannot submit to God's law, does not have the Holy Spirit living in him, has a mind set on the things of the flesh, and is living in rebellion and hostility toward God every day. I don't know that Thomas reaches moral crossroads as much as he *is* moral antipathy itself. Thomas has Libertarian freedom and can choose any course of action he wishes and has the power to do. As it is, Thomas, as a nonbeliever, will not desire 'the things of the Spirit.' He does not have the power to desire and act according to God's will. Regardless of whether he lost that power in Adam's fall or by his own first act of willful rebellion toward God; the fundamental issue is that he does not have it any longer. He is not spiritually free. Again, to be spiritually free is to have the desire and ability to live pleasingly to God; and Thomas does not have this."

Calvin: "Now, wait a minute! If Thomas, the nonbeliever, does not have the spiritual freedom to live pleasingly to God, then how can God hold Thomas accountable for his sinful actions? If Thomas cannot refrain from sinning, doesn't this mean that he is not responsible? Doesn't the same argument for Libertarian freedom (i.e. responsibility implies ability) apply to spiritual freedom as well?"

Wesley: "Good point, Calvin. This is something I, myself, was concerned about. Here's my answer to this: prevenient grace allows all nonbelievers the grace needed

---

motivational state in the action and their standing with Him (i.e. still in their rebellion). Thus, not only do nonbelievers lack the spiritual direction and ability to do the good in God's sight, but they also, due to their standing with God, are unable to transcend the category of sin. They can do nothing but sin.

to come to Christ and be saved at any moment. It is Christ's ever extended hand of salvation. Since Christians have the promise that they will always have enough God-given strength to refrain from sinning,[13] we can conclude that a nonbeliever has, at any moment, the opportunity to partake in this promise via faith in Christ, which is always near and available to her.[14] Thus, while a nonbeliever, *in her own power*, does not have the ability to refrain from sinning, she does have the opportunity to gain such an ability at any moment when she commits her life to Christ. Therefore, deadness in sin should point us to the fact that people need Jesus and not to giving up one of our clearest moral intuitions: '*ought implies can.*'"

Calvin, still pondering, gives Wes a slight nod and leans back in his chair.

Wesley: ". . . It is as Augustine once said, in referring to our sinful state, 'You are not blamed [before God] because you do not bind up your wounded limbs. Your sin is that you despise him who wishes to heal you.'"[15]

Rachel: "So . . . just to make sure I understand, professor. There are three issues at stake in the free will dialogue:

(1) Are we causally determined to act?

(2) Do we control our actions or are they random?

(3) Is there a freedom beyond just being Libertarianly free?"[16]

Wesley: "I could not have summarized it better, Rachel. This third point is a very important one. To be sure, when we become believers, we gain spiritual freedom. But as we mature in our faith, lean more on the Lord, become

13. 1 Corinthians 10:13

14. Romans 10:8–10.

15. Saint Augustine, *On the Free Choice of the Will*, (Englewood Cliffs: Prentice Hall, 1964), 128. See also John 3:18–20.

16. Romans 6:17, 18.

more in tune with his Spirit, and taste his goodness, our spiritual freedom grows. Until one day, when we leave this world and enter into glory, we will maximize this freedom, which means that we will have so much of God's strength, so much of his heart, and so much of his love, that sin will no longer be in the picture. We will still be Libertarianly free, but our spiritual freedom will so utterly remove sinful motivations from our 'reason-reserve' that they will no longer be a struggle for us. Only holy motivations will prevail."[17]

Rachel: "Wow! That really clears up a lot of questions. So, what does this mean for Reformed Theology, professor?"

Calvin gathered himself. He had learned so much this evening and was astounded at the twists and turns the conversation had taken. On the one hand, he felt humbled by the arguments and rebuttals that, before this evening, he had never dealt with. Yet, on the other hand, he felt a great welling up of passion; passion for the truth; passion to follow the Scriptures, logic, and his best prayer-infused reasoning to their proper ends.

Calvin: "The doors of Wittenberg, Rachel, do not swing from the rusted hinge of Compatibilism. No, no. *Sola Scriptura* is the threshold of the reformed house . . . . I suppose Reformed theologians, like myself, *may* need to reevaluate their conception of freedom and rethink some theological concepts. The jury is still out on that. But

---

17. One might ask, if we are unable to sin in heaven with spiritual freedom maximized, then how was Adam able to sin in the garden with his spiritual freedom maximized? My answer is that we will not be tempted in heaven. There will be no serpent and, hence, no possible motivations (whether internal or external) that could lead to sin. One could then ask, why did Satan sin initially? Without further information, I cannot say. Maybe Satan did not have spiritual freedom. Maybe there's more to the story that we do not know. I can say this, with what we know now, there's no firm answer.

fundamentally our hearts still burn with passion for God's glory. This will never change."

There was a long pause of silence. Each one thought to himself or herself on the entirety of the evening and on each of its salient points. Each one, baffled by the discussion's abrupt and providential turn, bore a look of sheer astonishment and joy for having taken part in such a wonderful dialogue. Wes rubbed his face in exhaustion and glanced into his coffee cup for more needed energy.

Wesley: "I guess we can call this a night, huh?"

Rachel: "Professors, thank you again for allowing me to join you this evening."

Upon hearing these words, Calvin's eyes now turned to Rachel's. She looked different to him now. Something had changed in his perception of her. No longer was she *just* the student; no longer was he simply the teacher. No, they were collaborators, equals, and fellow explorers in thick woods of metaphysics, both groping for the path to truth, both hoping that a warm and holy ray would grace their faces. This night, Rachel was the fountain of unexpected insight. Her contribution of that key passage – 1 Corinthians 10:13 – was pivotal to the subsequent discussion. She is *La Fontaine Inattendue*, that elusive and prophetic inkling Calvin had felt from entering the coffeehouse was now manifest in her. She, though externally just an inquisitive college student, would be the source of a revolutionary shift in paradigms for Calvin: *mankind is free.* He would, in time, change his philosophical system and reorder some of his theological beliefs, but he would never forget the girl who, though a humble student, toppled the parochial pillars of academia with one simple observation.

Coffeehouse Compatibilism

Further Reading: Theological Resources

Predestination and Free will: 4 views of Divine Sovereignty and Human Freedom

Further Reading: Compatibilism and Christianity

Martin Luther: *The Bondage of the Will*
Jonathan Edwards: *Freedom of the Will*
John S. Feinberg: *No One Like Him: The Doctrine of God* (Wheaton: Crossway books, 2001)
J.I. Packer: *Evangelism and the Sovereignty of God* (Downers Grove: Intervarsity Press, 1961)

Further Reading: Libertarianism and Christianity

William Lane Craig: *The Only Wise God* (Eugene: Wipf and Stock Publishers, 2000)
Alvin Plantinga: *God, Freedom, and Evil* (Grand Rapids: Eerdman's, 1974)

Epilogue

A Letter to Friends

O for a heart to praise my God,
A heart from sin set free. . .

—CHARLES WESLEY,
O FOR A HEART TO PRAISE MY GOD

Would you be free from your passion and pride?
There's pow'r in the blood, pow'r in the blood.

—LEWIS JONES,
THERE IS POWER IN THE BLOOD

DEAR READER, I HOPE you've enjoyed listening in on the dialogue of our three, or rather four, academics. I've actually hidden a fifth character in our dialogue. Can you guess who? Within the face and features of that unexpected source of insight lay the archetype of, well, you. She was your mirror and your personification in this story. She asked what you would ask and gave what you can give: real, paradigm-shifting, thought-provoking insight. So, be bold.

Epilogue

Be persistent. And never forget that your mind, your little questions and comments can be the fountain of big changes.

≈ ≈ ≈

You're surely asking yourself at this point, "What's the point?" Well, the point is, dear reader, there's a Berlin Wall traversing the open countryside of our theological land-scape; on one side reside the Calvinists and on the other the Arminians, and, unfortunately, there's rarely any discussion about the foundational, philosophical notions that under-gird each. After the debates in this book, I hope you can clearly see that there's *no middle ground* with Determin-ism and Libertarianism.[1] Either actions are agent-caused or they are not. In contrast, the goal of this book has been to create a middle ground or a safe place for Calvinists to check their philosophical baggage. Calvinists are largely Compatibilists[2] and, in my experience, feel they must be. It's a default position.

This book has challenged Compatibilist thinking to the core with the simple truth that our freedom in Christ, a foundational, theological truth, is incompatible with deter-minism. However, and purposefully so, I have not offered any direct arguments for or against any of the points of TULIP. Of course, as everyone else, I have my own ideas on each of the points. But my ambition in this work has been to plead with my Calvinist brothers and sisters to give up their Compatibilism/Determinism. It is an unbiblical and God-dishonoring dogma and does not fit the Calvinist's love for God, love for the truth of Scripture, and love for logic. I ad-mire my Calvinist brothers and sisters for their passion, but I plead with them now. Give up what is not worth keeping.

1 John S. Feinberg, *No One Like Him: The Doctrine of God* (Wheaton: Crossway books, 2001), p. 638.

2 Ibid., p. 638.

Break down the wall that divides us. Rebuild your lives and your theological system on the truth of Scripture: *human beings are Libertarianly free.*

www.ingramcontent.com/pod-product-compliance
Lightning Source LLC
Chambersburg PA
CBHW071101090426
42737CB00013B/2427